Understanding
Evil

Insights from Kabbalah

Jay McCrensky

Marketshare, Inc.
Bethesda, Maryland

i

Library of Congress Control Number: 2002111151

ISBN 0-9723672-0-9

Table of Contents

Preface

As human beings, we have been blessed with the gift of consciousness. We have eaten of the Tree of Knowledge. With the capacity to know and be aware comes the capability to create. We have become gods ourselves. We are creators of language, of societies, of nations, of solutions, of innovations, of technologies, of cures and of new life.

But, with the blessing comes the curse. With consciousness also comes death awareness, suffering awareness, evil awareness and the knowledge of and responsibility for right and wrong.

To cope with the curse we are given another gift, the gift of mysticism. We can feel, yearn for, experience spirituality.

This book provides a framework, a guide, and a foundation for that quest. It is a framework for contemporary intellectual, rational people, based on ancient wisdom handed down for generations and developed over centuries, called Kabbalah.

For the intellectual, scientific mind, Kabbalah offers a theological, ontological and cosmological system that is compatible with the Big Bang Theory of creation, with Quantum Mechanics, with evolution, and generally with most of modern physics, chemistry, biology and psychology. This book strives to revive the tradition, summarize the essence and take us a step forward in terms of modern day applicability and religious renewal.

The primary focus of this book, however, is the essence, source and manifestation of evil and sin. All modern religions to some extent try to guide us in dealing with evil in the world, misfortune and calamity affecting our lives, sin in ourselves, ethics in our decisions and the process of repentance toward making us better human beings.

For many individuals, however, dealing with sin is spiritually trying. From whom are we asking forgiveness? Why did we sin in the first place? Why is there sin and evil in the world? Why do we dedicate our lives to helping others and making a better world? What is the source of our creative or destructive potentialities? How do we define free will? These are questions many of us ask. We search for a framework for understanding the essence of evil and sin, as well as the nature of God, the purpose of human life and the role of religious observance in the larger picture.

The Kabbalah offers us a tradition of insight into these issues. This insight constitutes the foundation of Jewish mysticism. Kabbalah gives us a conceptual framework for understanding evil and enriching our notion of God and holiness.

In addition to helping us deal with evil, I hope this book provides an inspiring introduction to Kabbalah and new insights into the Bible and our religious traditions.

Acknowledgments

Understanding Evil is the result of many years of study, reflection and discussion. I owe inspiration to many, many people. Foremost among them are all the members of my religious Jewish community and havurah, Fabrangen, in Washington, DC. Key individuals to thank include my wife, Barbara, who did most of the typing, offered wonderful concepts and edits and served as an inspirational sounding board for new ideas. My friend and study partner, Simcha Guretsky, has made an invaluable contribution, both in editing the entire manuscript and in helping to develop ideas in the course of our years of joint study of the sources.

Finally I thank my many teachers, my parents, my 3 sisters and their husbands, my brilliant nieces and nephews and my children, Adam and Nathan, as sources of wisdom and understanding, compassion, strength, values and motivation.

Introduction

Evil and the Crisis in Spirituality

How can we pray to a god that let the holocaust happen? This is the crisis question of 21st century spirituality. How can we believe? How can we pray? How can we feel a oneness with the universe, a purpose in creation, a direction for life?

How can we explain the evil of bin Laden and a terrorist army, who, in the name of their concept of god, fly jets full of innocent people into buildings murdering over 3000. To the grieving families, friends, colleagues, how can we help deal with the tragedy spiritually? How could God let **this** happen?

How can we understand homicide bombers who enter buses, restaurants, crowded markets, private religious celebrations to blow themselves up while killing as many Israelis as possible? Where was God for **these** innocents.

How do we deal with utter self-centeredness, cruelty for pleasure, pure meanness, immorality, revenge, jealousy, murder? Why does God stand by? How can God allow evil to touch good people?

For many people the traditional answers of religious teachings are inadequate to answer these questions. Concepts of Satan, of evil inclinations, of a natural dark side to human nature appear theologically simplistic and spiritually empty.

But these are the questions we all ask. Can modern, intellectual, highly educated man and woman deal on a spiritual plane with their own and other's sins and with a god who allows evil to flourish and bad people to thrive? If we cannot find good answers and a foundation of meaning, the future portends the end of religion and perhaps of our ability to pray. There is truly a crisis in spirituality. Atheism is becoming the dominant "religion" of modern times, even among those who actively practice religious observance.

In Judaism, the crisis is particularly acute. Many who maintain a Jewish home, send their children to Hebrew and Sunday school, participate actively in temple or synagogue affairs and identify strongly with the Jewish people, claim not to personally believe in God. Many other Jews, even though from time to time feel intensely spiritual, nevertheless are troubled about believing on a rational level in a God who let the holocaust happen or who directed bin Laden's terrorists to destroy the World Trade Center.

Nonetheless, most of us do feel a divine presence. We feel spiritual. We experience a closeness to the divine. We pray. Perhaps, we push the problem of evil to the back of our minds. But the nagging doubt persists; **how can we believe in God after the holocaust and terrorism?**

This book addresses the above questions toward providing a framework for renewal of our spirituality and new meaning to our religious observances. The approach is not fundamentalist, but rather counter-fundamentalist. It is both philosophical and theological, both intellectual and mystical. It is Kabbalistic.

Kabbalah is a theosophy (a combined philosophy and theology) developed in the Jewish tradition, and adopted and applied in later centuries by a widespread Christian Cabala[1] movement. The name *Kabbalah* (a receiving) implies a handed down tradition. For centuries it was an esoteric body of knowledge, study and interpretive thinking, shared only among a fellowship of select rabbis and scholars. Some contemporary authorities claim that the basic conceptual framework developed in the 12th - 13th centuries when Kabbalistic writing began to appear; others claim Kabbalah developed as an oral tradition over centuries - from at least the 4th century and, perhaps, from biblical times.

The influence of Kabbalah is immense, though largely unrecognized. The concepts and framework influence modern psychology, literature, film and, of course, religion, particularly Judaism, in ways most are completely unaware.

Kabbalah influenced Hassidism, Carl Jung, and Shakespeare. However, it passed almost into obscurity in the 19th and 20th centuries due to a mistaken association with superstition, magic and

---

[1] Works by Christian Cabalists typically use this spelling. New age, occult oriented and Golden Dawn Qabbalists use a Q.

2

occult, some of which came out of Kabbalah. Thanks to such scholars as Gershom Scholem, contemporary spiritual leaders as Rabbi Zalman Schachter-Shalomi and contemporary creative writers and filmmakers, Kabbalah is being rediscovered. Kabbalah is opening new pathways to spiritual experience and connectedness to God.

There is one key aspect of Kabbalah, however, on which little has been written for contemporary readers - the potential to understand evil, sin and ethics theologically and religiously. This book addresses the problem of evil, sin and immorality based on the wisdom and concepts of the Kabbalah.

Evil as taught in the Kabbalah is a necessary byproduct of the human being's ability to create. The potentiality for evil, as the potentiality for good, has its source in God. God grants human beings the power and potential to be partners in ongoing creation. But if the creative potentialities and forces we receive from the unknowable source become out of balance, then immorality, sin and evil can result. The intelligence, powers and emotions we receive from God endow the potential for evil as well as good creation.

Chapters I and II outline the basic concepts and theosophy of Kabbalah to provide grounding for the discussion of evil in Chapter III. The concept of holiness is the focus of Chapter IV. Chapter V addresses and defines sin. Chapter VI develops the insights of Kabbalah toward a new philosophy of ethics as a basis for analyzing professional, legal, business and interpersonal ethical decisions. Chapters VII – XI apply these insights on ethics, sin and evil toward new understandings of *Genesis*. These chapters demonstrate how the Kabbalah can introduce new levels of interpretation and in turn how the *Five Books of Moses* helps us understand evil. Chapter XII provides a guide for applying this understanding of evil, sin and ethics to our own lives.

By the end of the book, I hope the reader can experience a gateway to Kabbalah, a wider appreciation of the wonder and depth of *Torah* and an intellectual foundation for religious renewal and spiritual growth.

Chapter I
Kabbalah: The Basic Concepts

Chapters I and II introduce the basic concepts of Kabbalah and set the stage for addressing evil in Chapter III. The study of Kabbalah is a lifelong pursuit. Key texts such as *Sefer Yetzirah*, *Sefer Bahir*, *The Zohar*, the writings of Isaac the Blind, Moses de Leon, Gikatilla, Abulafia, Cordovero, Vital on Isaac Luria, Luzotto, the Hasidic treatises and stories, and contemporary Kabbalistic thinkers, practitioners and renewalists, provide a never-ending wealth of complex, often contradictory, but inspired and inspiring material.

There are many perspectives and interpretations, for the tradition is often vague and obscure. There is no consensus understanding of Kabbalah, or of its various symbols, terminology and concepts. The diversity of the tradition opens worlds of opportunity for each of us to develop our personal understandings, our personal interpretation received from God that can be applied and useful for us in modern times.

Here is a summary of the basic concepts as I interpret them as most useful and insightful for understanding evil and experiencing an intellectually satisfying contemporary spirituality.

The Unknowability of God

We can feel the presence of God, the Shechinah, in Jewish observance and prayer, but we cannot define the ultimate source. We feel the high from a moving service. We feel God in the beauty and balance of nature. We feel an I-Thou closeness to the Almighty. We receive guidance and direction in our lives that we feel comes from God. But we cannot define or conceptualize God.

Kabbalistic writings repeatedly emphasize in poetic, symbolic and metaphorically wonderful ways, the fundamental unknowability of God, the source of creation.

Isaac Luria (the Ari) the famed 16th century forefather of the Kabbalah tradition, alludes to this unknowability as central to his whole cosmology. As his disciple Chaim Vital writes:

It is known that the highest light, above and beyond us with no end, is called the Ayn Sof. The name indicates that there is absolutely no way to comprehend Him, either by thought or by contemplation, because He is completely inconceivable and far removed from any kind of thought.[2]

The Zohar, the 13th century foundation work of Kabbalah, commences the Maamar Petah Eliahu:

You are He who is exalted above all exalted ones, mysterious above all mysteries. Thought cannot grasp you at all. (Tikune Zohar 12b).

Belief in God is thus a non-question for Kabbalists. One needs to have a conception of the divine in order to reject it. Once God becomes thought of as an unknown and unknowable source of the creative potential, rather than a being of some sort, based in mankind's image, the matter of belief is irrelevant

In a sense, Kabbalah can be thought of as counter-fundamentalist. God cannot be defined as a "being" of some sort because by definition we cannot know. Although God can have attributes, Kabbalah teaches we must endeavor to avoid trying to comprehend or conceptualize the ultimate source.

Evil is thus not predetermined or directed by God. Such a God who directs good and evil represents a conception of God, one the Kabbalists reject. Rather, the unknowable source emanates forces that enable us to create. But a condition of the power to create is the potential to mis-create. The source of creation is thus also the

---

[2] Chiam Vital, *The Tree of Life.*

6

source for the potential for evil and sin. This notion of evil is evil for which we are responsible, not the Unknowable.

Ayn Sof and the Many Names for the One God

The Kabbalists' name for the unknowable aspect of God is Ayn Sof, meaning without end, infinite. The concept of Ayn Sof implies *no end* to discovery, *no end* to the unknown, *no end* to creation. There is *no end* to the word of God. There is *no end* to interpretation and insight into God's words and doings. There is no end to good and there is no end to evil.

Infinity and unknowability are intimately related. We can create new knowledge by forging ahead in science, medicine, and astronomy; but ultimately there will always be a further unknown. Humankind will never stop discovering. We will never stop exploring new frontiers. We will never stop reproducing and creating a better world for our offspring and ourselves.

The various names for the divine force all have specific metaphorical and symbolic meaning in Kabbalah. Three names are important to differentiate here because of their key significance to understanding the Kabbalistic concept of God, unknowability and infinity.

Elohim refers in *Torah* to a generic sense of god with a small "g." It signifies the notion of god, the concept of god. In fact, it is plural in form and commonly referred to in *Torah* with the definite article, "the," as Ha Elohim (the gods).

Yod, Heh, Vav, Heh (YHVH), is the unpronounceable, holy name of the personal God of oneness. This is the concept of divine with whom we can have a mystical experience, an I - Thou relationship, with whom we can talk, hear and feel. The concept of holiness is associated with YHVH, but the name is so holy it is unpronounceable and thus "unknowable."

The **Shechinah** represents the presence of a spiritual force among us. But again it is a force or presence that, although we can feel and experience it, its essence is fundamentally incomprehensible.

Kabbalah thus gives us multiple names for aspects of the unknowable source. These include:

Ayn Sof - the unknowable, infinite source

Ehyeh - the source of becoming, of potentiality, of will, of inspiration

Yah - the source of wisdom

El - the source of kindness

Elohim - the small 'g', generic concept of divinity; the source of power and energy

YHVH - the unpronounceable, but personal divine we can experience and with whom we can communicate, the source of holiness, the essence of one-ness

Tzevaot - meaning hosts or forces, represents the aspect of God that directly influences us, who motivates, instills values, gives meaning and purpose to life

Shaddai - meaning "my breast," connotes the source of support, nurturing, faith, trust, satisfaction of our needs

The Shechinah - the aspect of God that "dwells" among us, whose presence we can feel.

Adonai - the ruler aspect of God that governs our daily lives, the sense of divinity we worship as Lord, offer thanksgiving, praise and make requests

Yet, even with these many names, and each signifying a class of forces or capabilities or manifestations, God is a unity. God unifies. God is harmony and balance. God is one.

Kabbalah as Personal Receiving

"Kabbalah," the Hebrew word, literally means a receiving or handing down. For centuries the Kabbalah was an oral tradition. In fact, the major works of Kabbalah assume a thorough understanding and grounding in this oral tradition and all of its related symbolism. To the uninitiated, the *Zohar* makes no sense.

Kabbalah comes essentially from God, the unknowable source, and is given to each of us. Our challenge and gift is to receive. We must discover our own personal Kabbalah, our own understanding and application. This book presents my understanding - you might accept some of it for yourself, you might reject some of it, but hopefully the material will stimulate in you the receiving process and the wonder and high of discovery and insight. This wondrous feeling is itself a gift from God, the unknowable source.

Just as each Jew must experience during the Passover Seder as if he or she personally was redeemed from Egypt by God, each of us can receive our personal Kabbalah. We must discover it and let God, through it, give our lives meaning, direction and joy.

The same holds for *Torah*. The Five Books of Moses given to the Jews at Sinai provide an inspired source of divine message. Perhaps the written *Torah* is a compilation of centuries of oral telling and retelling, divinely inspired; or perhaps Moses wrote it, directly interpreting his received message from God. We can never know and the answer doesn't matter. For *Torah* is given to each of us, and the personal message, our dedicated interpretation, is up to each of us to discover. As we gain insight from studying and discussion, we feel a special closeness to God, the unknowable source of understanding and insight, and can begin to personally feel and experience God's presence.

Torah is written in biblical Hebrew, an abbreviated, concise language, without punctuation or vowels. Each word can have multiple meanings. Different words can have the same or similar pronunciations. There is no break between sentences (no periods). Hebrew, more than most other languages, thus lends itself to multiple interpretation. We must each receive our personal interpretations by wrestling with, discussing, reflecting on, and listening to the text - and filling in the holes and gaps with our own stories. This is called *Midrash*.

As Bahaya Ben Asher wrote in the 14th century:

The scroll of the Torah is written without vowels, so you can read it variously. Without vowels, the consonants bear many meanings and splinter into sparks. That is why the Torah scroll must not get vowelized, for the meaning of each word accords with its vowels. Once vowelized, a word means just one thing. Without vowels, you can understand it in countless, wondrous ways. [3]

The Kabbalists believe Midrash continues in each generation in a process of continuous renewal. We are partners with God in creating *Torah* and discovering new understanding and meaning from *Torah*. God, the unknowable source, endowed us with the *Torah* as it is written and understood by previous generations. God also grants us the gifts of wisdom, understanding and inspiration to develop and discover our personal *Torah*. In chapters VI - X, I explore ways an understanding of Kabbalah and the Kabbalistic approach to evil can help us see new meaning in *Genesis.*

Creation and the God-Human Partnership

Although God is ultimately unknowable, we can receive energies and forces from the unknowable source that enable us to become partners with God in creation.

Creation to the Kabbalists is not a phenomenon that was completed in seven literal days. Rather, creation is ongoing. The process perhaps commenced in seven epochs or stages called Yomim (days) as elaborated in *Genesis* Chapter 1; however, creation continues. God (Ha Elohim) rested on the 7th day, a day that perhaps continues today, but evolution, expansion of the universe, and new creation continues.

Humankind's role is to partner with the Divine Source in continuing creation on earth and continuing discovery in the universe. The Jewish people in receiving the *Torah* have been given a special role as a "chosen" people. This mission is to help influence

---

[3]Translation by Daniel Matt, *The Essential Kabbalah*, Harper San Francisco, 1995, P146.

and direct ongoing creation in positive, rather than negative directions.

God needs humankind and the Jewish people, as humankind needs God. This symbiotic relationship enables discovery and creation. But humankind is an independent force in the creative process. We are extensions of God, but we are also free agents. We have free will. Hence, human-assisted creation and its resulting implications may not always be "positive." The role of the Jewish people is thus to help break the paradigms, introduce progress in every field of study and perhaps, most importantly, to serve as a force, a channel, for good. We are a *chosen people*, a special people with a mission to influence and balance creation for positive rather than negative, for good rather than evil.

Genesis is about the development of this partnering relationship between God, humankind and specifically the Jewish people. After the initial 6 days (epochs) of creation out of *tohu and vohu*, God leads all the animals before Adam as a second creation story. In this version, as Adam names them (discovers them), they come into being.

However, creation is far from complete according to *Genesis*. God (Ha Elohim) is not satisfied with his creation. The source of evil destroys it in a great natural disaster, a flood, but first, the power of God gives one man, Noah, the awareness, foresight and knowledge to build an ark to save his family and two of each animal.

Through partnership with Noah, God re-creates and re-seeds life on Earth. Yet, it's still not right. The new human societies unify and bond into a higher "organism" that said, "*Come together, let's build for us a city and a tower and its head in the heavens and we'll make for us a name (a god) lest we are scattered on the face of all the Earth.*" And YHVH responds, " *They are one people and one language, for all of them, and this they are beginning to do, and now nothing will stop them in doing all they imagine.*" (*Genesis* XI)

In response, in the Tower of Babel story God (Ha Elohim), the source of power and coalescence for good or evil, slows down the process of discovery, invention, engineering and human development by introducing a force of separation in humankind through multiple languages, tribes, and cultures. Only when and if humankind can

11

again unify, could it possibly build a figurative tower to heaven and reach Ha Elohim. Maybe the Internet is bringing us closer to that age as it reconnects all of us.

Chapter II

The Four Worlds and The Ten Sefirot

Although Kabbalah teaches that Ayn Sof is fundamentally unknowable, we can experience emanations of divine forces from the unknowable source. They endow to us a sense of divine outside and divine within. The flows enable us to live, grow, learn and create. They enable us to discern right and wrong, develop ethics, internalize values and derive principles. They give us energy, motivation and inspiration. These divine energies give us our ability to co-create in partnership with God. They provide the potentiality for evil as well as good; yet, without these forces, there can be no human creation - for either good or evil.

These flows are represented in *The Zohar* as streams or rivers of light, perhaps somewhat like flows of electrons, rays, or energies. We don't know and cannot know their essence; but we can receive, feel and define their presence.

They are called Sefirot. The word, Sefirah (Sefirot - plural) first appears in a mysterious ontological 2nd to 4th century work called *Sefer Yetzirah, the Book of Creation (formation)*. In its first chapter, translated below, Sefer Yetzirah defines key attributes of these mysterious forces, aspects that form the core of later 12th and 13th century writings. Kabbalists in the 11th –16th Centuries further reflected and meditated on the Sefirot. Through the Centuries rabbis assigned the Sefirot specific names, elaborated their essences and developed a complex framework of symbols, code names and correspondences.

Kabbalists employed these insights to discover new interpretations and messages from *Torah*, new levels of meaning and spiritual connection from Jewish prayers, and enhanced meaning from Jewish practices. The Sefirot became a framework for mystical techniques. The foundation for understanding the concept of Sefirot is contained in this short passage:

With 32 wondrous paths of wisdom, engraved Yah, YHVH, the Lord of Hosts, the God of Israel, the living God, King of the Universe, El Shaddai, Merciful and Gracious, High and Exalted, dwelling in eternity, whose name is holy. He is raised up and holy. And He created his world through three samach, peh, resh's[4]; through book (sefer), through number (sefar) and through telling (sepure).

Ten Sefirot, without what (of nothing, intangible). And 22 foundation letters: 3 mothers, 7 doubles and 12 simples. Ten Sefirot without what in the number of 10 fingers, five against five, with a single covenant mediating in the middle in a circumcision of the tongue and a circumcision of the sexual organ. Ten Sefirot without what, 10 and not 9, 10 and not 11.

Understand with wisdom and be wise in understanding. Comprehend with them and research with them and stand the word on its hole and seat the creator on his institution.

Ten Sefirot without what, their measure is 10 such that they have no end (Ayn Sof). Depth of beginning and depth of continuity; depth of good and depth of evil; depth of above and depth of below; depth of east and depth of west; depth of north and depth of south. The Master (Adon) will make unity. God, faithful King, rules all from his holy presence forever.

Ten Sefirot without what, their spiritual vision is like the view of a spark (Ezekiel 1:14) and their completion has no end (cutoff) and his doings (words of creation) through them are running and returning and his sayings (messages) are as a rushing wind. And before his chair they bow down.

Ten Sefirot without what, their end is buried in their beginning and their beginning, in their end as a flame linked to a burning coal that the Master (Adon) isolated. And he

---

[4]Three Hebrew letters, corresponding to s, f/p, and r. Together they form a root for related words having to do with communication.

has no second and before unity (oneness), what can you count (sofar).

Sefer Yitzirah thus teaches that these Sefirot:

(1) Are wondrous paths, created in wisdom, employed by the unknowable source to create, yield the various names and aspects of God that we can comprehend.

(2) Relate to the Hebrew root Samach, Peh, Resh, which form the words Book (Sefer), number (Mispar), and tell (Saper). These are the three primary forms of discovery, understanding and sharing of knowledge. The Sefirot represent the fundamentals of communication: written, mathematical and verbal.

(3) Are intangible, "without what." They are energies or forces, not concrete substances.

(4) Are10 in number, not 9 not 11, but precisely 10. There are ten categories of flow.

(5) Face, in two groups, as if on two opposing sides, with a mediating force equalizing and balancing between them. As we'll see, this has implications for understanding the essence of evil.

(6) They can be studied and meditated on, enabling us to approach the divine source and obtain mystical experience.

(7) They are infinite in depth, without end, and represent depth in all 6 directions. God provides the force of unity and balance and rules the flow.

(8) Are ever changing, dynamic, interacting and flowing in both directions.

As elaborated in the next chapter, these qualities of the Sefirot become important in understanding the source of and manifestation of evil as well as the nature of our creation partnership with God.

Based on this mysterious opening passage from Sefer Yitzirah, a millennium of rabbis and scholars meditated on, discussed, developed, interpreted, named and symbolized these ten Sefirot. In the 12th -13th centuries the Kabbalah took form, culminating in the appearance of the *Zohar* presented by Moses de

15

Leon in the late 13th century. The ever changing, dynamic, interacting, two way flowing relationship between individual Sefirot is a key focus of the *Zohar*. Their relative positioning provides insight and inspiration for understanding human potentiality and the creative process.

Through the centuries of oral Kabbalistic tradition, the ten Sefirot become each associated with different names of God and concepts of divinity. They become associated with various biblical personalities. They become symbolized by different colors. They refer to directions (north, south, east, west, up, down). They relate to different parts of the human body.

To decode the *Zohar*, the student must be aware of these alternate names, symbols, metaphors and associations. The *Zohar* is largely about these Sefirot, but seldom mentions them directly. The result is a hidden but exciting and dynamic meaning to the *Zohar* and, by extension, to the Kabbalah. This code of associations and referrals also keys to understanding *Torah* and the prayer book (siddur)

Knowledge of the Sefirot and their various appellatives also brings new meaning to the traditional Jewish prayers. Prayers such as *Lecha Dodi, Nishmat Kol Hai, the Alenu,* and the *Ayn Kamocha* come alive given awareness of the Sefirotic symbolism. Many of the poetic liturgy (piyutim) of the High Holiday prayer book, the *Machzor*, were composed by 11th to 16th century Kabbalists. They appear empty of meaning if one is unaware of the hidden Kabbalistic language.

The ten Sefirot are depicted and summarized in **Figure 1** (page 17, 109). Although they have been laid out in numerous configurations, orderings and relationships, this is the most traditional arrangement, called the **"tree of life."** The Sefirotic tree of life consists of four levels of Sefirot arranged in three columns with three sets of pairings. As you'll see in the next chapter, this intricate organization teaches us about the interrelationships of good and evil, the potentiality for sin, the philosophy of ethics and the spiritual balance for which we yearn.

16

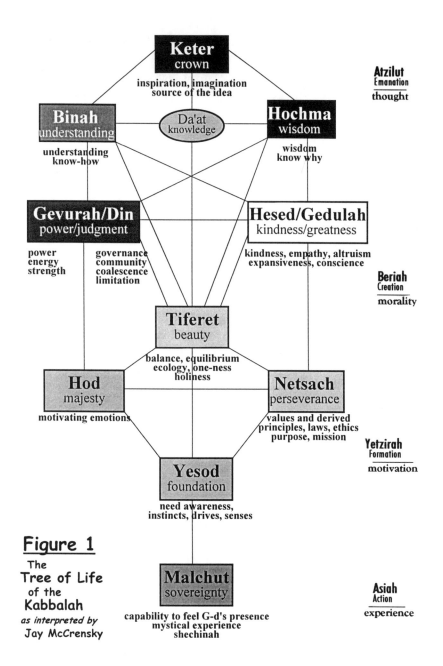

Keter
crown

inspiration, imagination
source of the idea

Binah
understanding

understanding
know-how

Da'at
knowledge

Hochma
wisdom

wisdom
know why

Atzilut
Emanation

thought

Gevurah/Din
power/judgment

power   governance
energy   community
strength   coalescence
               limitation

Hesed/Gedulah
kindness/greatness

kindness, empathy, altruism
expansiveness, conscience

Beriah
Creation

morality

Tiferet
beauty

balance, equilibrium
ecology, one-ness
holiness

Hod
majesty

motivating emotions

Netsach
perseverance

values and derived
principles, laws, ethics
purpose, mission

Yetzirah
Formation

motivation

Yesod
foundation

need awareness,
instincts, drives, senses

Figure 1

The
Tree of Life
of the
Kabbalah
as interpreted by
Jay McCrensky

Malchut
sovereignty

capability to feel G-d's presence
mystical experience
shechinah

Asiah
Action

experience

17

The Kabbalists, as inspired by Sefer Yitzirah, further define 22 paths, connections or relationships between the various Sefirot. These 22 paths are each associated with one of the 22 letters of the Hebrew alphabet. The 22 paths along with the 10 Sefirot became the foundation for the tarot cards.

From a contemporary perspective the Sefirotic tree seems to resemble the DNA molecule. Ironically, my first class on Kabbalah was held in a biology classroom. On the wall was a huge diagram of the double helix DNA molecule. One can't help notice the connection, not only in appearance. Like the Sefirot, DNA is the ultimate symbol of the potentiality of the coalescence of matter into increasingly complex forms. It is a symbol of the perfect balance of potentiality that maps a human being. It is evolved perfection and perfect balance. It is not in itself good or evil, but in its potentiality, it can be the source of both.

As depicted in **Figure 1** (see page 17, 109), the Kabbalistic tradition structures the Sefirot in four hierarchical levels. The four levels represent groupings of interrelated Sefirot. These levels are called *Olamot* (worlds) by the Kabbalists. Each level or world signifies an increasingly complex form of creative activity and evolutionary potentiality:

Asiyah (doing, making) - The level of experiencing, of receiving, of acting

Yetzirah (formation, creation out of existing matter) - The level of motivation to create, as stimulated by emotions, need awareness, values, and sense of mission or calling;

Beriah (creation from nothing) - The level of capacity for comprehending right or wrong, for decision making, for free will, for the power to create, for the conscience to judge our actions and for the potential for interpersonal relationships;

Atzilut (emanation) - The level representing our capacity for rational thinking, for analysis, for contemplation, for memory and for building knowledge.

The ten Sefirot and their grouping in the four worlds represent classes of creative partnering forces. They represent the full spectrum of capabilities and potentialities that enable us to partner with God in ongoing creation. Taking these one by one, below is a synopsis of there creative potentialities, along with the key associations with names of God, colors, directions, forefathers and body parts that are crucial to deciphering and understanding *Zohar* texts, Jewish prayer and many observances of the Jewish festivals, Shabbat and ceremonies. To explain the hierarchy of Sefirot, I start from the bottom of the tree of life (**Figure 1**, Page 17, 109) and work up.

The World of ASIYAH

Malchut – the capacity for mystical experience

The lowest level of the Sefirot, receives the flow of forces from all of the higher Sefirot. Asiyah (meaning being or doing) is the level of experience and action. It is the level of our day-to-day creative actualization. It is the sphere of reception and implementation of our creative impulses, ideas and motivations.

Asiyah includes but one Sefirah: **Malchut** (translated sovereignty or kingship). **Malchut** comprises humankind's capacity to feel divine presence, to experience God, to have a mystical experience. The primary name of God associated with **Malchut** is the Shechinah. In Judaism, the Shechinah, a feminine aspect of the divine, is always in our midst; we need only to reach out, recognize, and receive by creating the appropriate environment or context. To Kabbalists it is female in the sense of receiving the seed from above, of gestating and nurturing the embryonic creative potential and of birthing creativity.

Environments that enable a feeling of closeness to God, that call forth the Shechinah, might, for example, involve prayer, Tefilin observance, lighting the candles to usher in a holiday or Sabbath, *Torah* study and the many other observances, practices and traditions of Judaism. Meditation and other universal tools of the mystic can also bring forth the Shechinah. Kabbalists have devised a wealth of meditation techniques toward achieving a oneness with the Shechinah and potential for raising through the Sefirotic realm closer to the divine source.

People also experience closeness to God apart from any particular religious observance or activity. Suddenly, perhaps in a time of crisis or intense emotional need or ecstatic happiness, we just feel God's presence. We might experience a beautiful scene on a mountain, a quiet moment on the beach, a moving sense of closeness with a child or lover and feel that the Shechinah is present.

To Kabbalists, the capacity to experience/feel God is itself a gift from God and even, perhaps, an aspect of God. It is the essence of spirituality. It gives us meaning to life and the capacity to be and do - to exist and to create. This is **Malchut**. This is the force of the Shechinah. This is God-awareness in the creative process and creation partnership that comprises the level of **Asiyah.**

The code names and appellatives in Kabbalistic writings and prayers are numerous for **Malchut**. These appellatives and metaphors are summarized in **Figures 2 and 3** (pages 21 & 23). The *Zohar* and other Kabbalistic works use these symbols as a sort of poetic code, rather than the direct names of the Sefirot.

Sabbath is a key appellative and metaphor for **Malchut** in the *Zohar* and other Kabbalistic texts. Adonoi, in addition to Shechinah, is a name of God reference for **Malchut**. King David, the builder and sovereign, is the forefather associated with **Malchut**. Rachel, Miriam and Esther also reference **Malchut**. The feet, liver and mouth are areas of the body connected by various Kabbalists to **Malchut**. The oral law and our ability to communicate and pass down knowledge are integral aspects of **Malchut**, as is our ability to experience and express a connective ness to God. The direction associated with **Malchut** is west, the direction of the sea when in the holy land. West is the direction that Jonah fled from the mission of God. Blue, the color of royalty, is the **Malchut** color. The moon, which reflects the light of the sun, influences our emotions and internal clocks and serves as the basis for Jewish time keeping, is the heavenly body associated with **Malchut**.

FIGURE 2
DECIPHERING THE ZOHAR AND OTHER KABBALISTIC WORKS
Metaphors, Symbols and Appellatives

The Sefirot: Colors, rivers, heavens, supports, worlds, aspects, borders, hosts, levels, powers, sides, areas, lights, garments, steps, crowns, foundations, streams, gates, the Garden of Eden, the chariot, field of apple trees, Adam Kadmon.

Keter Hochma, Binah: The undisclosed.

Hesed, Gevurah, Tiferet, Netsach, Hod, Yesod: The six days, the sun, the Lebanon, vav.

Hesed to Yesod [in some writings, **Hochma** to Yesod]: Ze'ir Anpin (the impatient one, the small face)

Simeon Bar Yohai: Sacred lamp.

Keter (crown): King, black, no color, will, nothingness, well, Israel, most hidden One, hidden upper light, most mysterious, Arikh Anpin (the patient one, the large face), ancient of days, Ehyeh (I will be), Atika Kadisha (ancient holy one).

Hochma (wisdom): Yod, dark blue, father, husband, first point, beginning (reshit), brain, Yah.

Binah (understanding): First heh, green, mother, wife, sea, palace, basin, womb, heart, brain, inner voice, Leah, YHVH vocalized as Elohim.

Hesed (kindness), Gedulah (greatness): Upper waters, white, south, right arm, Abraham, Miriam. hasid, El.

Gevurah (strength), Din (judgment): Lower waters, red, north, left arm, fire, wine, the evil serpent, the accuser, the tempter, Isaac, Elohim.

21

Tiferet (beauty), Rehamim (mercy): vav, Holy One Blessed be He (Hakadosh Baruch Hu), Holy King, yellow, son, sun, torso, heart, east, wind, tree of life, written Torah, prince, central pillar, central column, Jacob, YHVH.

Netsach (victory, endurance): the right leg, Moses, Rebecca, YHVH Tzevaot.

Netsach and Hod: the two pillars, willows of the brook, testicles.

Hod (majesty): the left leg, Aaron, Sarah, Elohim Tzevaot.

Yesod (foundation): Tzadik (righteous one), kol (all), phallus, Joseph, Tamar, moon, Shaddai, El Hai.

Malchut (sovereignty): second heh, community of Israel, Shechinah, queen, Sabbath, the female, bride, princess, the daughter, moon, blue, west, great sea, speech, oral Torah, end of thought, lower mother, tree of knowledge, apple orchard, Kind David, Rachel, Miriam, Esther, Adonoi, *Tzedek* (righteousness), Tzedakah (charity), liver, feet, mouth.

FIGURE 3
THE METAPHORS, SYMBOLS AND APPELLATIVES
BY THEME

As a study and deciphering guide, following is a summary of Sefirotic associations (as used by various Kabbalists) organized by theme.

The Forefathers and Mothers

Abraham **Hesed**	Isaac **Gevurah**	Jacob **Tiferet**	Joseph **Yesod**
Moses **Netsach**	Aaron **Hod**	David **Malchut**	Solomon **Hochma**
Sarah **Hod**	Rebecca **Netsach**	Rachel **Malchut**	Leah **Binah**
Miriam **Malchut** **Hesed**	Tamar **Yesod**		

Divinity Names

Ehyeh **Keter**	Ha Makom **Keter**	Yah **Hochma**	YHVH Elohim **Binah**
El **Hesed**	Elohim **Gevurah**	YHVH Tzevaot **Netsach**	Elohim Tzevaot **Hod**
Shaddai **Yesod**	El Hai **Yesod**	Adonoi **Malchut**	Shechinah **Malchut**
YHVH **Tiferet**			

The Family

Father **Hochma**	Mother **Binah**	Son **Tiferet**	Daughter **Malchut**

23

Areas of the Body

Brain	Heart	Right Arm	Left Arm
Hochma	**Binah, Tiferet**	**Hesed**	**Gevurah**
Crown of Head	Torso	Right Leg	Left Leg
Keter	**Tiferet**	**Netsach**	**Hod**
Right Brain	Left Brain	Genitals	
Hochma	**Binah**	**Yesod**	
Feet	Mouth	Liver	
Malchut	**Malchut**	**Malchut**	

Royalty

King	Queen	Prince	Princess
Keter	**Malchut**	**Tiferet**	**Malchut**
Holy King			
Tiferet			

Colors

White	Red	Black	No Color
Hesed	**Gevurah**	**Keter**	**Keter**
Yellow	Green	Dark Blue	Royal Blue
Tiferet	**Binah**	**Hochma**	**Malchut**

Letters of The Name (YHVH)

Yod	Heh	Vav	Heh
Hochma	**Binah**	**Tiferet, Yesod**	**Malchut**

Heavenly Bodies

Sun	Moon
Tiferet	**Malchut**

Directions

North	South	East	West
Gevurah	**Hesed**	**Tiferet**	**Yesod, Malchut**
Gevurah/Hod/	**Hesed/Hochma/**		
Binah	**Netsach**		
Up	Down		
Keter	**Malchut**		

Days of the Week, Days of Creation

Sunday Day 1	Monday Day 2	Tuesday Day 3	WednesdayDay4
Hesed	**Gevurah**	**Tiferet**	**Netsach**
Thursday Day 5	Friday Day 6	Shabbat Day 7	
Hod	**Yesod**	**Malchut**	

The World of YETZIRAH

HOD		NETSACH
	YESOD	

Yesod – Need Awareness

In this next higher Sefirotic level, we begin to receive flows that are crucial to enable our co-creator roles. It is the level of motivation to create.

The 9th Sefirah is called **Yesod**, translated as foundation or basis. But, as with all the Sefirot, it signifies much more than the literal translation of its name.

Yesod is motivation associated with our God-given drives, instincts, and senses. God endows us with an innate ability to recognize, feel and experience our needs. We are blessed with the gifts of sight, hearing, smell and touch; and with the capacity to feel hunger, thirst, cold, and heat to assure our very survival. God also gives us the direct capacity to create new life, to reproduce through our sexual drives.

Yesod in the Kabbalah thus encompasses the full range of motivation related to need awareness: our sexual drives, our thirsts and hungers, our physiological needs, our psychological needs, our instincts for survival. We share many of these with other animals. The **Yesod** force is not unique to humankind. God enables survival of all life through the forces of **Yesod**. However, as the psychologist Abraham Maslow has conceptualized, human beings are also driven by higher categories of need. These include needs for safety and security; affiliation and recognition; self-esteem; and self-actualization. Maslow's hierarchy of needs are further manifestations of **Yesod**. God motivates us to be creative, to partner in creation, through our awareness of, recognition of and experiencing of these higher level, more complex needs, as well as our basic drives and instincts. In Chapter VI this concept is developed and applied to understanding Noah and in Chapter IX, to Joseph.

The two names for God associated with **Yesod** are Shaddai and El Hai. Shaddai literally means "my breast" in Hebrew. As Rabbi Mordechai Gafni has pointed out, the essence of faith (emunah) is the complete trust of a baby that it won't be dropped as it nurses (nursemaid is omain in Hebrew from the same root as emunah). Through **Yesod** we have faith in God that our needs will be satisfied. Shaddai, and by implication **Yesod**, is God's breast. Through **Yesod**, God is our milk maker. Just as manna was provided in the desert, God metaphorically makes the milk, provides the nourishment we can receive in **Malchut**. El Hai means "God of life." Through Yesod, God endows the need awareness that enables life and the reproduction of life.

The Kabbalists also address **Yesod** as kol (all, everything). Kol connotes that we can experience God in everything, a sense of pantheism. There is holiness and the essence of God in everything if we can be open and receive and recognize. Everything comes from God, and through the filter of **Yesod**, can reach us in **Malchut**. In a sense, all our needs are a reflection of divine essences. There is some aspect of God in any need we can experience and by which we can be motivated.

In *The Zohar* and other Kabbalistic writings, Noah and Joseph are associated with **Yesod**. The sexual organs are the associated body parts and the associated directions are westward, toward the sea or downward toward the earth.

> *...Through his prayers, one should bring El Hai into Adonoi ... When the attribute Yesod, which is called El Hai, is bound to Adonoi (**Malchut**), then one can draw down all his needs.*

Joseph Gikatilla, Shaarei Orah, 14th century

Hod - Motivating Emotion

Of all the Sefirot, least appears in the tradition about **Hod** (majesty). Nonetheless, it is crucially important in understanding the source and manifestation of evil. As the eighth Sefirah, it is positioned above and to the left of **Yesod** (see Figure 1, page 17, 109).

Hod represents our ability to receive and manifest motivating emotions. Emotions enable us to survive. Our emotions make us "human," but do not alone differentiate us from lower animals. Certainly, canines, apes, dolphins and other mammals display intense emotions. They help bind societies, protect our families, reward our accomplishments, and define our pleasure and displeasure. Emotions are necessary to sustain motivation and provide stick-to-itiveness as well as the impetus to begin. Without emotion, there can be no sustained creation.

Through **Hod**, God endows us with emotions that we can experience as positive, negative or neutral. Emotions of a positive or pleasurable nature include passion, excitement, love, enjoyment, and curiosity. How often do we act or create simply for enjoyment, because it's fun. Love motivates us to protect, nurture and assist. Curiosity is the impetus to discovery.

More neutral motivating emotions might include anxiety, loneliness, frustration, guilt, shame, and boredom. Loneliness can motivate us to find companionship. Guilt and shame (or avoidance of) motivate men to fight or to take action. Anxiety causes us to take steps to relieve the anxiety, solve the problem. Boredom keeps us active and learning.

The source of the capacity for negative and unpleasant emotions is also in God. These include such feelings as remorse, fear, anger, jealousy, disgust, hurt, and insult. Feeling sorry is a strong motivator to take corrective action and to repent. Fear protects us. Anger motivates reaction and vengeance. "I'm mad and I'm not going to take it anymore," can be a sufficiently strong impetus to finally take action. Jealousy fosters protectiveness and competitiveness. Hurt, insult and disgust motivate action to feel better, action to undo or assuage the intensity of these strong feelings.

The Hebrew word *Hod*, literally meaning majesty, is related to the word for thankfulness (**Hoda**'ah) and the word for echo (hade). It also is the core of the word Yehudah (Judah), Leah's fourth child, but the first for whom she felt true thankfulness and connection to God. Thankfulness is truly an emotion, a feeling, if it is genuine. Just as an echo, our emotions reflect back to us from those who receive them and we naturally echo back the emotions we sense from others.   Love brings on love; anger generates anger; remorse stimulates remorse.

It is a powerful spiritual concept to recognize that our motivating emotions and feelings stem from flows and energies whose source is divine.   Everyday we should thank God for these wondrous, essential, complex feelings.   Emotions make life pleasurable or painful, are the essence of our personalities, and give us impetus to act, to solve, to repent and to create.

Netsach - Motivating Values, Purpose and Mission

The 7th Sefirah, completing the triad of the world of Yetzirah, is **Netsach** (meaning victory, endurance, perseverance). As for **Hod,** the essence of **Netsach** is far beyond the literal meaning of the name.   What gives us "victory," what enables us to "endure" are our motivating values and the ability to derive and discern principles, mores, ethics and laws from these values.   **Netsach** is our God given ability to discern values and derive principles.

The unknowable source emanates our ability as human beings to receive, internalize and act on values.   Not everything we call values are necessarily God sourced.   What we define as values or principles could easily be corrupted by our emotions or self-interest.   Nevertheless, it is a powerful concept that our fundamental ability to receive and be motivated or influenced by values comes from a higher source. This side of motivation, our ability to act on values coming from God, is the essence of **Netsach.**

The book, _For Cause and Comrades - Why Men Fought in the Civil War,_ by James M. McPherson, crystallizes the essence and power of our values and principles as motivators.   McPherson raises the questions: what is it that motivates men in battle to charge forward to certain death; what holds the military unit together in such a way that men are motivated to risk their lives and perhaps face certain death.

Studying Civil War letters, McPhearson draws some fascinating conclusions about the role of values.   McPhearson finds that patriotism, duty, and obligation to family motivated soldiers to enlist and sustained them into battle in the Civil War.   Primary group cohesion, intense feelings of responsibility to comrades, kept them fighting and dying. This group cohesion was based on deep-set values that human beings seem to hold naturally.

Values and the ability to derive principles and mores from them are essential to our living in families, tribes and societies. The values that we have the ability to derive from **Netsach** combine with **Hod** emotions to enable humankind to collaborate, team, and coalesce into more powerful organisms. These higher organisms, which we call families, tribes, societies and nations, enable and motivate higher and higher levels of creation. Advances in medicine, communication, transportation, computation, technology, construction, economics depend on an ethical, principled, value-driven foundation. Without the capacity for values, we face antagonism and opposition rather than collaboration and teaming. Animals also seem to be endowed with innate values, as well as emotions. The loyalty of a loving dog to its master can lead to truly heroic acts. Protectiveness of an animal of its young is value-driven, not simply instinct.

God enables and influences the process of partnering in ongoing creation by bestowing values and the principles, ethics, laws, and teachings we derive from values. God's influence and guidance through **Netsach** might be categorized as follows:

> **Society and community enhancing values** include humility, duty, honor, loyalty, justice, open-mindedness, flexibility, and altruism.

> **Personal mission enhancing values** include concern for others, *tikun olam* (fixing the world), liberalism, progressiveness.

> **Perseverance enhancing values** include stick-to-itiveness, commitment, and responsibility.

> **Interpersonal relationship building values** include honesty, integrity, friendship and generosity.

Values, like emotions, are complex. Some appear learned and others innate. Kabbalah teaches that the ultimate source of our capacity to receive and internalize our values is divine. This capability for guiding values (**Netsach**) and motivating emotions (**Hod**) is a flow of force, **Tzevaot**, from above. The name **Tzevaot** is the appellation for God associated with **Netsach** and **Hod**. **Netsach** is **YHVH Tzevaot**; **Hod** is **Elohim Tzevaot**. Perhaps the angels of heaven (referred to as the Tzevaot) are figurative forces that help us receive both values and emotions and through this, instill motivation.

To some Kabbalists, *Torah* as a process is associated with **Netsach**, for *Torah* is the essence of and ultimate symbol of our receipt of values and the derived principles and law from God. Similarly, some Kabbalists perceived **Netsach** as representing the source of prophetic revelation[5]. *Torah* and prophecy communicate the laws and practices that provide a foundation for Jewish religious belief and observance. *Torah* and prophecy convey universal values and encourage principles and ethics based on these values. *Torah* means teaching. It is a vehicle for God to speak to us, both as a community and personally as individuals. *Torah* is an embodiment of the emanation, **Netsach.**

The Shema, the core prayer of the Jewish faith, has a special meaning in connection with **Netsach.** We pray "Shema Yisroel" ("Hear Israel") in every service (as a reminder that our ability to receive values and derive principles comes from God. We are reminded how Moses implores in Deuteronomy, " Hear Israel," the values, the laws, the ordinances flowing from God.

The Sefirah **Netsach** also embodies the sense of mission or calling that human beings have the capability to receive. We can receive direction, purpose and goals, just as values, from God. Our sense of mission is essentially a personal articulation of our values and priorities. Religion often helps us connect with and formulate a life purpose and meaning. These are the forces of **Netsach** at work.

The forefathers symbolizing **Netsach** and **Hod** are Moses and Aaron respectively. Moses, the prophet, the lawgiver, the principle-maker, the mission motivator is a name for **Netsach.** Aaron the emotion-

---

[5]Schaya, Leo, *The Universal Meaning of Kabbalah*, Penguin, 1958, p. 56.

director, the reconciler, the echo, is a symbol for **Hod.** The body areas associated with **Netsach** and **Hod** are the right and left thighs or legs. *The Zohar* speaks of them as pillars. Truly, **Netsach** and **Hod** are the motivational pillars on which our creative potentiality stands. Emotions and values and missions are the legs on which we walk forward. They enable us to move in new directions. They are the candlesticks and candles holding the flame of the higher Sefirot.

The World of BERIAH

GEVURAH/DIN	**HESED**
TIFERET	

Tiferet (beauty) – Balance, Equilibrium

The 6th Sefirah, **Tiferet** (beauty), is central to the entire realm of the 10 Sefirot. It represents the forces of balance, centeredness, oneness, unity, equilibrium, ecology, homeostasis - all the concepts of harmony and balance in the universe, in humankind and in ourselves.

Evolution has brought about a wondrous balance among the diversity of life on the earth. The environment provides a perfect balance to sustain life. Our human bodies are finely tuned balances of cells, organs, systems and hormones. If we become out of balance, we become sick. Kabbalah thus provides a spiritual definition of sickness. *Tameh* is the Hebrew used in *Torah* to designate a state of spiritual impurity. In essence, it is a state of loss of balance, physically or emotionally. *Tameh* is thus a state of heightened potentiality for sin.

Our relationships require balance to thrive and grow. We must constantly work at maintaining a balance of love, principles, emotion, restriction and freedom in relationships with spouses and lovers, with children, with friends, with relatives. **Tiferet** gives humankind the potentiality of interpersonal relationships that work, grow and create.

32

Our communities, societies and organizations also thrive and grow through a balance of rule/law and openness/freedom. Healthy, vibrant societies and organizations effectively balance competing interests, needs and wants. The balance of supply and demand drives our economies. Capitalism serves as the engine of economic development when the economy achieves the right balance between free enterprise and regulation, and between business ethics and the profit motive.

Tiferet represents the diverse forces from God, both physical and spiritual, that promote homeostasis and the maintenance of or return to or establishment of balance.

In *The Zohar* and other Kabbalistic writings, one name for God associated with **Tiferet** is *The Holy One* or *The Holy One, Blessed be He/She.* This central Sefirah in the Tree of Life symbolizes holiness and blessings; it implies a fundamental relationship between holiness and balance. The Kiddush (sanctification over wine), that traditionally commences each Jewish holiday, literally means "making holy". Using wine, the symbol of power, we are bringing our powers into balance and becoming "centered" as we create holiness in the Sabbath or holiday and in ourselves in celebration of it. The Hebrew word for marriage (Kiddushin) also comes from the word for holy (Kadosh). Marriage is a uniting of two souls into a relationship of perfect balance, or holiness. We are creating a holy context for creation partnering with God.

Another name of God associated with **Tiferet** is the tetragrammathon, Yod Heh Vav Heh (YHVH). This is the unpronounceable name of God, the personal name of the God we can experience mystically, the name of God used in *Torah* in conjunction with personal mystical experiences and a direct communication relationship with God. When God directly relates to the forefathers and mothers, God is known as YHVH. This is the holy name of God.

The central prayer of the Jewish service, the Shema, is all about **Tiferet**. *Hear Israel: YHVH is our God(s) (Eloheinu); YHVH is oneness (unity)* is a summation of **Tiferet**. Oneness is not an abstract concept in Kabbalah, it has specific spiritual meaning. *"YHVH is One,"* the central Jewish expression of belief in one God, is also about **Tiferet**, the Sefirah of unity and balance. Recognizing that balancing forces are emanations or flows from the unknowable source (Ayn Sof), gives **Tiferet** a special place in our spirituality. Oneness or centeredness is the nucleus of our creative potentiality. We strive for a oneness, a perfect balance, in ourselves, in our relationships and in our communities.

The balancing forces of Tiferet interact with and mediate between the other Sefirot. We can mystically effect a merger, an intercourse, between **Malchut** and **Tiferet** and bring holiness into ourselves. To Kabbalists, this is the central goal of prayer. On a left-right plane, we can experience **Tiferet** as a force for balance between **Netsach**/values, **Hod**/emotions and **Yesod**/need awareness. Tiferet enables a perfect balance of divine motivation.

Tiferet also represents balance in the world of Beriah, the Sefirotic level of awareness of and responsibility for right and wrong. In the *Genesis* creation story, Adam and Eve achieve the level of Beriah in the evolution of human development in the act of tasting the red[6] apple of the tree of knowledge in the center of the garden. In *The Zohar*, the garden is an appellative for the Sefirot as a whole. The *tree of knowledge in the center of the garden* represents **Tiferet,** located in the center of the 10 Sefirot.

Unlike any other animal, humankind has been given the capacity for establishing and maintaining equilibrium in ourselves and in the world. **Tiferet** thus also serves as a balancing force between the two Sefirot immediately above it on the Tree of Life, **Hesed** and **Gevurah.** Together the three represent our awareness of and responsibility for good and evil.

The forefather associated with **Tiferet** is Jacob. Its corresponding heavenly body is the sun. Its color is yellow, like the sun. Its corresponding body area is the torso (to some Kabbalists, the heart). The direction of **Tiferet** is east, toward the holiness of Jerusalem and the rising sun. Other symbols include son (of **Hochma** and **Binah**), wind, written *Torah*, prince, central pillar (column), and holy king.

---

[6]The color red and the snake are Kabbalistic symbols of **Gevurah**, discussed below.

Gevurah - Power (Also called Din - Governance)

The fifth Sefirot has been given two names in the tradition. Its essence can be thus understood as a complex interplay of its two names: **Gevurah** and **Din.**

Gevurah is the power, strength, and energy for creation. **Din** represents the natural coalescing and bonding forces of nature. **Din** enables and encourages human beings to coalesce, build relationships and unify into larger, more powerful organisms called societies.

The two names each signify a different but related side of the Sefirah. On the one hand, God, Ayn Sof, grants us the power **(Gevurah)** to create. This might be in the form of strength; in the form of our arm, hand and fingers; in the form of financial means; in the form of influence over or leadership of others. Such power is a necessary condition for creative partnering.

The **Din** (relationship/governance/judgment) nature of this Sefirah represents our God-given capability for relationships that give power over others. This power of governance and judging is the force that enables governments, nation states, universities, corporations, associations, communities and families. Through communities, we magnify our ability to create; without them we are limited to our own bodies and minds. **Din** enables division of labor, collaboration, specialization and the exponential creative potentiality of the larger organism called society and civilization. It is the force that drives the coalescence of human beings into more powerful creating organisms.

Gevurah/Din represents this ultimate force of coalescence. The unknowable Ayn Sof combines and organizes atoms into molecules and molecules into compounds. Ayn Sof coalesces matter into galaxies, stars, solar systems, and planets. Human beings are actually highly organized colonies of cells. Our cells are organizations of complex molecules. On another plane, this force from Ayn Sof coalesces humankind to form families, clans, tribes, societies, and countries.

While **Tiferet's** association is with YHVH, the personal and holy name of God, **Gevurah/Din** is associated with the name Elohim. A plural construction, Elohim can be understood in *Torah* as god with a small "g." It is the more abstract, non-personal, concept of divinity. In its association with **Gevurah/Din**, Elohim represents the power of creation and coalescence, the capability to be a creator or co-creator and the forces ("gods") that unify us through governance into ever more productive and powerful communities.

Gevurah/Din represents the side of YHVH that brought the Jews out of Egypt, out of bondage, out of the narrows, to freedom. It is the side of YHVH that gives us the power to revolt, to free others, to fix or improve the world. It is the energy and strength for Tikun Olam (the Kabbalistic concept of the Jewish people's mission to fix or better the world).

A Jewish holiday celebrating **Gevurah/Din** is Passover (Pesach). We consequently lean to the left, the side of **Gevurah/Din** (see Figure 1, page 17, 109), while drinking wine, a symbol of **Gevurah/Din**, at the Passover seder. Hamatz (non kosher for Passover food that Jews avoid eating during Passover) represents the "evil inclination," the uncontrolled potentiality of **Gevurah/Din**. Jews thus symbolically eliminate the evil inclination in avoiding *hamatz* in order to celebrate the power-giving side of God: the God who brought the Jews out of Egypt with a mighty hand and an outstretched arm. We are told to experience the Seder as if we personally were brought out of Egypt. We have been given the responsibility to receive and harness this power to use for creating a better world. At the same time, however, we must strive to control the evil inclination related to raw power.

Yom Din, the Day of Judgment, is Yom Kippur. This day of **Din** is both a celebration of our partnership with God in channeling the power of ongoing creation and a day of Judgment of our personal success or failure, and thus of our sinfulness, in exerting that power (**Gevurah/Din**).

The color of **Gevurah/Din** is red (the color of wine and blood). The direction is north (for conquering armies came from the North). The body area is the left arm and hand. The forefather association is with Isaac. Other appellatives include the evil serpent, the accuser, and fire.

Hesed - Kindness (also called Gedulah (greatness))

Hesed, Hebrew for loving kindness, as a Sefirah represents all the good inclination forces we possess. The Sefirah, **Hesed**, encompasses goodness, beneficence, kindness, compassion, altruism, and the capacity for empathy. **Hesed** gives human beings the capacity to feel another's pain. It represents our innate desire to do good. **Hesed** is the source of our yearning to help others. It fuels our desire to make a better world.

Hesed, as a flow from the unknowable source, endows us with a natural inclination toward goodness in our creativity and our actions. It is truly an aspect of God working within us.

As indicated in Figure 1 (page 17, 109), **Hesed** flows into **Netsach**, influencing our sense of mission and life goal. It influences our ability to receive values and how we derive principles and law. Note that **Netsach** is positioned directly below **Hesed** on the right side of the tree. This positioning is highly significant as discussed in Chapter III.

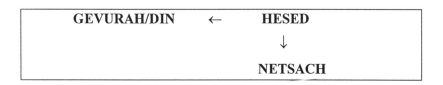

Also significant is **Hesed**'s positioning on a plane next to **Gevurah/Din.** The kindness factor, Hesed, also flows from right to left, into **Gevurah,** and serves as a crucial balancing force to **Gevurah.** There is a dynamic flow between the two Sefirot and a crucially important balancing role played by **Tiferet.** With **Hesed** alone, we cannot create; with **Gevurah** alone, the creation will be devoid of positive purpose or good intention. Kindness, compassion and love are wonderful essences, but they are passive essences. They cannot alone bring about a better, more compassionate and loving world. They require a partnering force, **Gevurah**, to effect change and enable creation. It takes power, **Gevurah**, to bring about a kind action.

Like **Gevurah/Din**, **Hesed** has an alternate name: **Gedulah** (greatness, largeness). **Gedulah** connotes a great force, harnessing and countering **Gevurah/Din**. On Passover the matzah represents **Hesed/Gedulah** as the great harnessing counter force to **Gevurah/Din**. Leaven or *Hamatz* represents the evil inclination. We eat matzah instead as a symbol of the purity and goodness of **Hesed**. Perhaps George Lucas's "force" in Star Wars is a reference to the force of Gedulah, the counter force to the "dark side" or **Gevurah**/Din. *"Let the force be with you"* could be taken to mean: let your natural inclination to kindness, goodness and altruism overcome your natural inclination to self-centeredness, egoism and self-interest.

The God-name for **Hesed** is El. Its color is white. Its forefather is Abraham. South is its direction. The right arm and hand is **Hesed**'s associated body area. Other appellatives used in the *Zohar* include upper waters and hasid (a pious man of kindness).

The world of Beriah is now complete. It is a balanced unity of **Hesed** (goodness) and **Gevurah/Din** (power/governance) through **Tiferet** (balance and centeredness). Together with Yetzirah, the world of motivation, humankind is endowed with the potential to maintain and sustain and build upon God's creation. Human beings can partner in ongoing creation with God.

Five of the six central Sefirot, **Hesed/Gedulah**, **Gevurah/Din**, **Tiferet**, **Netsach** and **Hod,** take their names directly from the *Torah* service. We sing from the Biblical Book *Chronicles*, as we march the *Torah* around the synagogue, *"Lecha YHVH ha Gedulah ve ha Gevurah ve ha Tiferet ve ha Netsach ve ha Hod"* – "To You YHVH is the **Gedulah** and the **Gevurah** and the **Tiferet** and the **Netsach** and the **Hod**." The passage then continues, *"Ki'chol bashamayim uvaaretz lechah YHVH hamalacha"*- "For **all** in the heavens and on the earth is yours, YHVH the **kingdom**." All is a code name for **Yesod**. The kingdom references **Malchut.**

The six from **Hesed/Gedulah** to **Yesod** are referred to as the Vav (meaning 6) of the name, Yod Heh <u>Vav</u> Heh (YHVH). They represent the six days of creation, the six days of the work week (Shabbat is associated with **Malchut**), the six directions (north, south, east, west, up, down), the six forefathers (Abraham, Isaac, Jacob, Moses, Aaron, Joseph), and the bridegroom of the Shechinah (**Malchut**). (An alternative numbering scheme starts with **Hesed** as one and thus corresponds to the weekday relationship. **Keter, Hochma and Binah** become 8, 9 and 10. Thus, be careful in interpreting Tarot cards.) See **Figures 2 and 3** (pages 21 & 23) for a summary of the appellatives, symbols and metaphors associated with the various Sefirot.

The World of ATZILUT (Emanation)

	KETER	
BINAH	**(Da'at)**	**HOCHMA**

The top triad of Sefirot constitutes the world (olam) of Atzilut. This level of creative force represents the potentialities of intelligence, knowledge, analysis, inspiration, ideas, reasoning, conceptualization and wisdom. The world of Atzilut consists of three distinct Sefirot: **Keter** (crown), **Hochma** (wisdom) and **Binah** (understanding). Merged together in balance, they enable the creation of knowledge **(Da'at)**. **Da'at** is positioned in the central column. It designates a product of **Hochma** and **Binah**, but is not itself a stand alone Sefirah. Let's look at each Sefirah separately and at the relationship between them.

Binah – Understanding, Intelligence

Binah literally means "understanding" but also has the same root as the verb to build. This third Sefirah from the top represents our intelligence and our ability to use intelligence to build (boneh) knowledge. I think of it as "know-how." It is our ability to receive information, process information, remember and discover. **Binah** represents our capability to comprehend, to realize, to visualize, to plan and ultimately to *understand.*

39

Without **Binah**, humankind can build nothing. God created **Binah** to enable ongoing creation with we humans as the partner with God. In isolation, **Binah** can generate ideas, plans, know how, but not a physical product. At a minimum, it requires **Gevurah/Din** as the energy and **Hod** as the motivation. Given sufficient power (**Gevurah/Din**) and emotional drive (**Hod**), combined with the understanding of how to plan and carry it out (**Binah**), humans have been given the potential for nearly unlimited construction.

The story of the Tower of Babel (*Genesis*-XI) demonstrates the potential of **Binah, Gevurah/Din**, and **Hod** (understanding, power/governance and emotional drive) to give humankind ultimate creative capability.

> *And it became that all the earth was one language and one doings. And it came to pass in their traveling from the East (Tiferet), they found a valley in the land of Shinar and lived there. They said man to his neighbor, "Come let us make bricks and burn them thoroughly". Brick served them as stone and they had material for mortar. And they said, "Come, let us build* (from boneh) *for us a city and a tower with its head in the sky. We shall make for ourselves a name; else we shall be scattered on the face of all the world." YHVH came down to see the city and the tower that the humans built. And YHVH said, "They are one people and one language completely, and this is what they begin to make and now nothing will block them of anything that they intend to make. Come let's go down and there confuse their language so that one man will not hear the language of his neighbor." And YHVH scattered them from there all over the earth and they stopped building the city. Thus it is called there confusion* (Babel) *because YHVH confused the language of the whole earth, and from there YHVH scattered them on the face of all the earth.* (Genesis 11:1-9)

In this short nine-line story, humankind has evolved its **Binah**, introduced just above in the Noah story, to the point that YHVH fears the results of unlimited **Binah** potential. The world is also totally unified *(all men migrated from the East; else we shall be scattered; as one people with one language)* signifying unlimited **Din**. But YHVH (**Tiferet**) fears that humankind is not yet ready for full, unified intelligence. God thus introduces "confusion" (the root of the word Babel) as a tactic to limit or slow the potentiality of **Binah** and **Din.**

In the *Zohar*, **Binah's** metaphor is a mother, the mother of creation. **Binah** is like a womb, gestating ideas received from the two upper Sefirot until they become know-how, until they are understood, until the information becomes knowledge.

The *Zohar* code names for **Binah** in fact include such terms, as *mother, womb,* and *sea.* **Binah** metaphorically gestates and births the lower Sefirot (discussed above). Out of **Binah** comes the six channels/rivers leading to the lower six Sefirot and ultimately to **Malchut.** **Binah** is thus the "mother" of all lower creative God-partnering forces. **Binah,** the essence of our God-given ability to think, is an incubator.

With respect to the body, **Binah** is associated with the heart and also with the left side of the brain, the side of logical, rational thought. Its God-name is YHVH with the vocalization of Elohim. It is represented by the first heh of YHVH. Other appellatives in the literature associated with **Binah** include palace, basin, inner voice, Leah and the color green.

Hochma – Wisdom

Hochma is more transient, more amorphous, and less tangible than **Binah.** It represents that fast flowing, hard to define essence we call wisdom. In contrast to **Binah** as know-how, **Hochma** is know-why. It tempers and directs **Binah** so the resulting knowledge (**Da'at** - represented as a mediation or balance between them) is positive, useful and directed.

Wisdom is an innate ability God gives us that enables us to recognize higher meaning and to see deeper significance. Wisdom enables us to break paradigms. Wisdom enables us to recognize new solutions, to solve seemingly impossible problems with new insight. Wisdom enables us to see below the surface to the essence of the thing.

In another sense, **Hochma** represents our ability for abstract conceptualization. Primate scientist Daniel Povinelli of the

41

University of Louisiana has found that abstract conceptualization is beyond a chimp's ken. In essence, our ability for abstract conceptualization is what truly differentiates humans from all other animals and what most makes us god-like. **Hochma** thus incorporates our ability to think about thinking. It is a transceiver to receive inspiration from the Source. It is our ability to receive messages through *Torah*. It is our ability to receive and discern meaning in Kabbalah.

Without **Hochma**, human beings can still build, tapping **Binah** and **Gevurah/Din**, but the product will be a Tower of Babel - a useless product of human energy and unity. Perhaps the pyramids are examples of such building devoid of higher purpose, that in no way betters society or the welfare of humankind. A powerful, hierarchical civilization developed the knowledge and technology and mustered the slave power to create one of the seven wonders of the ancient world. Yet to what purpose? With what wisdom?

Reflect for a moment. You can probably think of people who are highly intelligent, yet seem to lack the amorphous, transient quality we call wisdom. Perhaps they can memorize and learn and remember, but seem weak on the ability to conceptualize abstractly, to see the larger picture, and to break out of the box. Without **Hochma**, their empty intelligence cannot really serve them as a true partner with God. As discussed later in reference to ethics, foolishness is the opposite of wisdom.

The Zohar visualizes **Hochma** as a stream that seeds or impregnates **Binah**, the female, the *mother*. **Hochma** is correspondingly referred to as *father*. It is a current, shaped like a *Yod*, flowing into the sea, like semen into the womb fertilizing the egg. This is the birth process of creation. The Yod of Yod Heh Vav Heh symbolizes **Hochma**. The name of God in association with **Hochma** is Yah. Isaac Luria referred to **Hochma** and **Binah** as Abba and Imah (father and mother) because they fertilize, gestate and give birth to the lower Sefirot. Other appellatives of **Hochma** include husband, first point, beginning (Reshit), and brain.

God gives us wisdom; God gives us understanding. Together, they give us the potential to create knowledge, to learn, to be conscious. This product is what the Kabbalah calls **Da'at**. **Hochma** and **Binah** represent the two hemispheres of the brain.

42

Hochma is the right side, the side of intuitive and creative thought. **Binah** symbolizes the left side, the side of rational, analytic thought. In balance together, the left and right hemispheres enable us to better think, discover, compose, articulate and remember.

Keter (crown) – imagination, inspiration

The highest Sefirah, the first and topmost Sefirah, is called the crown, **Keter**. To some Kabbalists, **Keter** is synonymous with Ayn Sof, the unknowable source. Others (including me), however, prefer to think of **Keter** as the first receiving Sefirah from the unknowable source above. As indicated on **Figure 1** (page 17, 109), **Keter** is positioned as part of the central column at the top.

In the creation process **Keter** represents what comes before the intangible flow we call wisdom/**Hochma**. To me, it is the inspiration and imagination that becomes the source of the new idea. Einstein reportedly said that imagination is more important than knowledge. **Keter** is the imagination of which Einstein refers. It is positioned directly above **Da'at** (knowledge) in the hierarchy of the tree of Sefirot. As Einstein understood, many people demonstrate intelligence and understanding, fewer add real wisdom to this **Binah**. And very few have the true ability of imagination enabling the creation of new concepts and paradigms out of nothing.

In Zohar, **Keter** is the source of the current of **Hochma**. **Keter** precedes *Reshit*, (an alternative name for **Hochma**) meaning the beginning, of creation as a process. It is the B' of B'Reshit, the "In" of "In the beginning Elohim created the heaven and the earth."

The concept that there is a force from God that precedes our wisdom, understanding and very consciousness has deeper implications. Kabbalah thus teaches that our inspiration and imagination come from God, from the highest level closest to the source itself. Unification with this unknowable force beyond consciousness is the ultimate goal of many Jewish mystics through meditation and other techniques.

Keter is referred to by some Kabbalists as Ayin, nothingness. It is as if ideas come from a void of nothingness, a state of pure meditative receptivity. Imagination is free form daydreaming on nothingness.

There is something spiritual in inspiration. To be inspired is a tremendous gift. How many highly creative writers, musicians or scientists try for years to compose or discover but get nowhere. Despite depth of wisdom and depth of understanding, their creative juices require some amorphous nothingness we call inspiration. Then suddenly from nowhere it comes, the creative process is opened and creativity flows like a river.

Keter is also associated in Kabbalistic writings with "will" (ratzon). It represents the will of Hashem to create, the fundamental purpose of life. It also represents the divine manifesting in our own personal will as connected to, or a part of, or a reflection of the will or purpose of God. Our impetus or desire to create comes from the power of the source, the will of **Keter**.

The God-name for **Keter** is *Ehyeh,* meaning I will be. The future connotes potentiality and the creation to come. Said another way, the potentiality of future creation is the will of God. The associated color of **Keter** is black, since it reflects no light, but is the source of all light. Other *Zohar*ic names and references include King, well, Most Hidden One, hidden upper light, and most mysterious. Isaac Luria referred to **Keter** as *Atika Kadisha* (the ancient holy one) and *Arikh Anpin* (the patient one).

Summary of the Sefirot

We have now defined all ten Sefirot.

Flowing downwards from the highest level, creative potentiality from Ayn Sof starts with **Keter**: the will to create and our own receptivity to the will of God as expressed or sensed in our personal will. Creation starts from the ultimate and indefinable source of our inspiration that enables the whole creative process.

- The flow descends to the level of creative knowledge building: **Hochma** - the know-why, the wisdom to direct and steer and feed the gestation of knowledge; and **Binah**

- the know-how, the comprehension of how to gestate knowledge;

- The flow descends to the level of moral responsibility: **Hesed,** goodness, compassion and altruism; **Gevurah,** power and the capability for societal governance; and **Tiferet,** the balance, unity and oneness of perfection.

- The flow descends to the level of motivation: **Netsach,** values and derived principles; **Hod,** emotional motivation; and **Yesod,** our drives, instincts and awareness of needs.

- The flow descends to the level of receptivity and experience: **Malchut,** from which we receive the sensitivity to feel the presence of God and to experience spirituality.

Creation comes from God. Through creation we are partners with God. God needs us; we need God.

The quote below from the *Zohar* presents a poetic summary for this chapter. It is one of the few places in *Zohar* that actually mentions the Sefirot by name.

> *From this we may determine: One is the source of the sea. A current comes forth form it making a turn, which is Yod. The source is one, and the current makes two. Then the vast basin known as the sea is formed, which is like a channel dug into the earth, and it is filled by the waters flowing from the source; and this sea is the third thing. This vast basin is divided into seven channels, resembling that number of long tubes, and the waters go from the sea into the seven channels. Together, the source, the current, the sea, and the seven channels make the number ten. If the Creator who made these tubes should choose to break them, then the waters would return to their source, and only broken vessels would remain, dry, without water.*

> *In this same fashion has the cause of causes derived the ten aspects of Himself, which are known as Sefirot and named **Keter** and the source, which is a never-to-be-exhausted fountain of light. Consequently, he designates*

45

himself Ayn Sof, Without End. He has neither shape nor form, and no vessel exists to contain him, nor any means to comprehend him. This is referred to in the words, 'Refrain from searching the things that are too hard for you, and desist from seeking for that which is hidden from you' (Ben Sirah from Talmud, Haggigah 13a).

*Then he shaped a vessel small as the letter Yod. He filled it from him and called it **Hochma**-gushing fountain, and called himself wise because of it. And then, he formed a large vessel named sea and designated it **Binah** and himself understanding on its account.   He is both wise and understanding in his own essence.   However, **Hochma** in itself cannot claim such a title, but only through him who is wise and has made it full from his fountain; thus, **Binah** in itself cannot claim that title, but only through him who filled it from his essence; it would be turned into an desert if he were to withdraw from it. In this respect it is written, 'As the waters descent from the sea, and the river is drained dry' (Job 14.11).*

*Finally, 'He smites the sea into seven streams" (Isaiah 11.15).   That is, he directs it into seven precious vessels which he calls **Gedulah, Gevurah, Tiferet, Netsach, Hod, Yesod, Malchut.** In each he designates himself thus: great in **Gedulah**, strong in **Gevurah**, glorious in **Tiferet**, persevering in **Netsach**, 'the beauty of our maker' in **Hod**, righteous in **Yesod** (Proverbs 10.25). All things, all vessels, and all worlds does he support in **Yesod**. In the last, in **Malchut**, he calls himself King, and his is 'the **Gedulah**, and the **Gevurah**, and the **Tiferet**, and the **Netsach**, and the **Hod**; for all that is in heaven and in earth is for you; for you is the kingdom, YHVH, and you are exalted as head above all' (Chronicles 29.11).*

In his power rests all things, be it that he chooses to reduce the number of vessels, or to increase the light issuing from them, or the reverse. But over him there exists no deity with power to increase or reduce. (Zohar II, 42b)

Evil, as discussed in Chapter III, is an unfortunate but necessary potentiality in this process of receiving the Sefirot.

Chapter III
The Source of Evil and Sin

Chapter II lays out the basic conceptual framework for the 10 Sefirot. But they are not constants; they are a dynamic energy, perhaps like an atom or molecule. As described in *Sefer Yitzirah*, the Sefirot are many-faceted and in continual interaction and flux. They interact, combine, and exert influence one against the other. The Kabbalists have brilliantly defined and depicted these dynamic forces in the structure of the *tree of life*, Figure 1 (page 17, 109). As Figure 1 portrays, the ten Sefirot divide into four horizontal levels (Atzilut, Beriah, Yetzirah, and Asiyah), and stand in three columns, a right, a left and a central column.

In the right column are **Hochma**, **Hesed** and **Netsach**. On the left are **Binah, Gevurah/Din** and **Hod**. And in the center, mediating between right and left, are **Keter, (Da'at), Tiferet, Yesod** and **Malchut**.

Left Column	*Center Column*	*Right Column*
	Keter	
Hochma		Binah
Gevurah		Hesed
	Tiferet	
Hod		Netsach
	Yesod	
	Malchut	

Given the dynamic and interactive nature of the Sefirot, the process of creation can be highly volatile and unstable. The *Midrash* teaches that God perhaps created several worlds before Earth. Finally, the creation process on Earth became one with which God was truly satisfied, one that He saw as "good." *Genesis* then recounts the continuing creation process, as God attempts to direct and influence Earth development.

First, God intercedes to introduce confusion into **Binah** to limit or slow humankind's creative potential in the Tower of Babel story. Then, God once again recognizes evil and tries to wipe it out with the Flood; and, finally, God directly interjects a third time to influence ongoing creation and development on Earth by the appointment of the Jewish people with a special mission to guide from within. Even God has difficulty controlling the process of creation.

Perfect creation requires perfect harmony, perfect balance, perfect equilibrium - otherwise the result is something short of *"And it was Good."* Creation is dynamic process. The output, the created result is ever changing, ever evolving, moving in and out of balance. We can build a perfect house - but over time the elements, settling, wear and tear bring our perfection into disrepair. We've got to constantly maintain, fix and restore to keep our creations in a close approximation to the balance that was originally declared in *Genesis* I to be *"good."*

As partners with God in ongoing creation, human beings have responsibility to continuously strive to maintain balance and constantly endeavor to hold the world around us in balance. Human beings have a role in homeostasis. The Jews in particular, as a chosen people with a mission of *Tikun Olam*, have a special role in restoring and fixing (tikun) balance. The central column, **Keter**, (**Da'at**), **Tiferet**, **Yesod** and **Malchut**, enable us to do this.

The Sefirot of the right side provide seeds and sperm to impregnate the womb of creation on the left.

Hochma seeds **Binah**;

Hesed seeds **Gevurah**;

Netsach seeds **Hod**.

As described in *The Zohar,* Wisdom **(Hochma)** is truly a wondrous sperm flowing into the womb of Understanding **(Binah).** This womb or sea of understanding can then gestate the seven lower Sefirot. Kindness **(Hesed)** similarly seeds power/coalescence **(Gevurah/Din)** to guide and direct the creative forces of **Gevurah.** Our values and principles **(Netsach)** flow into a sea of emotions **(Hod)** to give us motivation, without which there can be no creative product.

But the right side in isolation cannot produce a creative result. Without the creative force of the left side, there can be no creation. Wisdom, goodness and values do not in themselves "create," just as the male cannot create without the female.

Thus, the Kabbalists refer to the right column of Sefirot as the "male" Sefirot and the left side as the "female "Sefirot. This is a <u>sexual</u> metaphor, not sexist. The groupings are "male" and "female" in the sense of seed, impregnation, womb and birthing - not in the sense of masculine or feminine characteristics.

However, the left Sefirot, if combined, have the potential to create without any input from the right. **If that happens the result is pure evil.** Power, sustained and motivated by raw emotions, in combination with intelligence, but totally lacking wisdom, compassion, and values, results in evil.

If the Sefirot become out of balance, if we become out of balance, the left-side Sefirot, those of understanding without wisdom, power without empathy, emotions without values, the result is sin. If human beings manifest the pure potencies of **Binah** (understanding or intelligence) in combination with **Gevurah/Din** (power and control over others) and **Hod** (emotions to motivate), but void of any mediation or counterbalance from the right side, we have the more intense evil of al Qaeda, Nazi Germany, Rwanda and Cambodia.

Bin Laden, Hitler, Pol Pot, Haman and Amalek can be understood as manifestations of the forces of the left. In the literature of Kabbalah, the left side of the Tree of Life has become understood as the source of the forces of evil. This power has been referred to as the *sitra ochra* (the other side), the *yetzir ha rah* (the evil inclination, literally, evil creation), Samael (the angel Satan, from *smol,* left), the "dark side" (of *Star Wars*), the sinister (from the Latin for left hand).

Did God allow the Holocaust? Could God have intervened? We can now address such questions. Through the Sefirot, human beings are endowed with the potential to be co-creators. History is not determined or controlled by God. Rather, human beings are an essential force to develop Earth. But the potentiality for genocide is a necessary condition. Without the forces of the left there can be no creation at all. This potentiality also has its source in God as the origin of understanding, power and emotions.

But, God also gives us the capability to defeat evil. God also gave humankind the compassion, wisdom, values, emotions, power and intelligence to stop holocausts and defeat Hitlers.

To further clarify the implications and gain insight from the left - right relationship, let's explore the "male-female" dynamics one level at a time.

The Binah-Hochma Dimension

Binah, out of balance with **Hochma**, means pure intelligence without sufficient wisdom to direct and temper it. **Binah** is know-how, the knowledge to build; but without wisdom, isolated intelligence can result in misdirected, warped product. There is little **Hochma** mixed into the understanding of how to build more efficient human extermination technologies. **Netsach** without **Hochma** results in false values and missions, the foolish rationalizations of evil perpetrators.

Technology itself is morally neutral. It is the degree of wisdom directing the development and use of that new technology that determines good or bad, the productive or destructive, the progressive or retrogressive results.

In today's high technology world there are abundant examples of intelligence without wisdom. Internet technology short on wisdom can produce web sites that share illicit knowledge, such as bomb-making know-how, or reinforce extremist or terrorist communities and other manifestations that are destructive rather than expansive. Genetic engineering without wisdom can mean blind experimentation with uncertain results, maybe resulting in new viruses; or other forms of monsters. New technologies that we apply without adequate testing (wisdom) can endanger rather than improve and save lives. New pharmaceuticals brought hastily to market can kill rather than heal.

Evil acts, defined so by virtue of their result in human suffering and death, are always rationalized by their perpetrators. Ted Kaczynski rationalized that his bombings would some how bring down the hated technological society. Timothy McVeigh claimed he was fighting the loathed Government and avenging Waco, all "for the larger good," as he stated it. Suicide bombers and other terrorists believe the murder of Israeli children will somehow help their own people and lead to eternal heavenly bliss for themselves. These acts all resulted from individuals exercising **Binah**, but lacking **Hochma**. They defined their own values, principles and missions out of a corrupted **Netsach**, due to absence of **Hochma**. They were blind to the foolishness of their acts, a foolishness that is so transparent to the rest of the World.

A prime example of evil resulting when **Hochma** is absent is mob violence. When the flow of **Hochma** is cut, the mob rules. A mob cannot reason, cannot evaluate, cannot conceptualize, cannot grasp the wider significance of their action or the moral implications. Rather, they are driven by raw emotions, the power of the gang and lynch party rationality. A mob feels no empathy for the victims. The results are the atrocities in Rwanda, the ethnic cleansing and gang rape in Bosnia, the pogroms in the Ukraine.

The Gevurah-Hesed Dynamic

On the level of Beriah, the interplay is between **Hesed** and **Gevurah/Din**. This dualism constitutes the central dynamic of Yom Kippur. We pray for God's **Hesed** that forgives and pardons, rather than His **Din** that judges and punishes. At the same time, we are praying for our own **Hesed** to temper our **Din/Gevurah**.

Gevurah is the power to create. **Din** represents the creative power of coalescence into communities. Raw evil results if **Din/Gevurah** dominates **Hesed**, our inclination for goodness and altruism and our ability for empathy. But, goodness and altruistic intention cannot in isolation, independently create. We need strength/energy. But, unfortunately, raw power isolated from **Hesed** produces evil.

The evils of tyranny result from unadulterated power. The evils of slavery come from power over others without mercy (**Hesed**). Societies and nations enable human progress and growth, but they also can produce despotism, ruthlessness, and selfish tyranny.

The perpetrators of evil acts all share a lack of any capacity for empathy with their victims. This void of compassion renders them unable to feel the pain or terror of another. They cannot see themselves in others. This is a manifestation of the total absence of **Hesed.**

A void in **Hesed** makes it possible to de-humanize the other, a manifestation of a void from **Netsach.**

On Yom Kippur we traditionally wear white, the symbolic color of **Hesed**, as a reminder of our need to temper our own power with loving-kindness. We remind ourselves in the *Vidui* (confession prayer) of our failings in our own God-given **Gevurah**. We ask how we can fulfill our mission as co-creator and partner with God by strengthening our God-given **Hesed**, as a balance to **Gevurah.**

On Passover, Jews remove and avoid *chamatz* (leavened products from yeast) from their homes and their lives. Chamatz is the symbol of the *yetzir ha rah*, the evil inclination (literally, the evil creation). Matzah, on the other hand, symbolizes **Hesed**. Yeast can produce leavening for bread, but too much, results in spoilage.

Passover is a festival celebrating the positive potentiality of **Gevurah**. At the seder, as we drink four glasses of wine, a symbol of **Gevurah**, we lean to the left. It is God's outstretched arm and strong hand, additional **Gevurah** symbols, that brought us out of Egypt. In the *Hagadah*, Rabbi Eliezer, Rabbi Joshua, Rabbi Elazar ben Azariah, Rabbi Akiba and Rabbi Tarfon sat all night telling of the departure from Egypt. Night is another reference to the left side in the Kabbalistic tradition. Rabbi Elazar then elaborates that he did not understand why the telling of the departure from Egypt is at night until Ben Zoma expounded that the Biblical commandment to remember the going out of Egypt all the days of your life includes the nights also. Between the lines is the implication that revolts are planned at night. The Rabbis mentioned were the very rabbis who planned the Bar Kochba revolt.

The message of the seder becomes clear: In every generation we must each experience the power of being freed from Egypt, and we must partner with God to bring freedom to others. We must harness and balance the potentiality of **Gevurah** toward building more just societies, without servitude or any other forms of human degradation or exploitation.

This is *tikun olam*, the Kabbalistic concept of fixing and restoring the world. This is the mission of the Jewish people. Passover teaches us about the **Gevurah - Hesed** balance; how to use our **Gevurah** to reach out to **Hesed** and together with **Hesed**, with Matzah and without Hamatz, to build better societies.

The Hod - Netsach Interplay

On the level of Yetzirah, we experience the dynamic dualism between **Netsach** and **Hod** - our values and our emotions. Again, as for the two above levels, there is a tension between right and left. On this level of motivation, we can be driven to act primarily from the right, from our values and value-derived principles, mission, purpose goals; or, we can react and respond from the left, through our emotions. Emotional motivation is essential to survival, for we would not act without the impetus provided by our emotions. If we react only emotionally, however, we open a potential for sin. We become less human, more animal-like. We make mistakes we later regret - for we acted without thinking, without values, without principles. We acted emotionally.

The biblical concept of *"Tameh"* (spiritually impure) bears on the **Netsach - Hod** continuum. In *Bamidbar* (The Book of *Numbers*), we are warned of the state of *Tameh*. We are defined as in a state called *Tameh* when we are emotionally vulnerable - when our emotions may overcome our principles, our mission. *Tameh* is defined as occurring in menstruation, in sickness, around death and mourning (the touching of a body). The cure is for the *Tameh* individual to be separated from the community, isolated from the potentiality of Din. In periods of *Tameh*, God is saying, "Be careful!

Watch your emotional motivations! Remind yourself of and strengthen your principles!"

Moses (the forefather representing **Netsach**) becomes *Tameh* in Bamidbar on the death of Miriam, his sister. Consequently, immediately following, he strikes the rock for water rather than talking to it; he then personally claims the credit for bringing water out of the rock. Unlike Joseph who credits God as the source of the power he manifests to interpret dreams, Moses in his anger and frustration takes personal credit. As a result, God bans Moses from crossing into the promised land.

Moses, also in a state of *Tameh*, orders the slaughter of the Midianites. This act of vengeance becomes an evil holocaust in every sense. In this controversial and mysterious passage, Moses commands the conquering Israelites,

> *"Arm from among you men for war. You will give the vengeance of YHVH on Midian." (Numbers 31:(3)). The Israelites slew every male (31:(7)). ...And the Children of Israel took captive the women of Midian and their little children ...(31:(9)). Moses was enraged with the officers of the soldiers ... Moses said to them, "You let live the women? ... Now kill all male children and kill every woman who has known a man that has slept with a male, kill. And all the small female children that have not slept with a male, let live for yourselves."*

The above is a literal translation of a section of *Torah* we don't study in Sunday school. Even Moses our teacher can exhibit evil. Moses was *Tameh*, vulnerable, and succumbed to his emotions and his power.

As the text states, *"Moses was enraged with the officers."* Why? *Torah* gives no explanation: certainly, the officers did nothing ostensibly sinful or disobedient. The explanation is in Moses' emotional state; his emotions are subordinating his values and the principles and morality that stem from those values. The value of human life, the mission of creating a people, the values relative to teaching and law giving are overwhelmed by emotions of grief, of anger, of frustration, of impatience. And Moses is the symbolic forefather name for **Netsach**! *Torah* is teaching that we all have the potential for evil if we allow our emotions to override our values.

The basis of racism and prejudice is the innate survival-based tendency human beings have for hostility toward strangers. These emotions of innate hostility to anyone not part of our identity group facilitate the dehumanizing of the opposition, the competitor, and the unfamiliar. Such emotions enable evil acts. Without countering values that accept the stranger, that welcome the unfamiliar and recognize all human beings as one family, the emotions of racism and ethnic hatred predominate.

Both anti-Semitism and anti-Americanism stem in part from deep seeded jealousy. If the Jews are seen as rich, smart, and privileged, people hate Jews. America today is becoming the "Jew" of the world. The al Qaeda message is rooted in hatred for the United States in part because Americans represent wealth and well being in contrast to the poverty of the third world. The al Qaeda goal of destruction of America and the tactic of murdering Americans represents a Nazi like "anti-Semitism" rooted in jealousy, expressed through hatred, absent of values.

If there is a void of divine **Netsach**, groups and communities like al Qaeda teach their disciples that people of another country, race, ethnic group or religion are sub-human, are the cause of your suffering, are out to get you, must be destroyed before they destroy you. This is the foundation for war. Without **Hochma** and **Hesed** in **Netsach**, ideologies are misleading, values become warped and principles are false.

Children commonly commit horrendous acts we could define as evil (teasing, tormenting, injuring others) because they literally don't know any better. Their moral development (**Netsach**) lags, possibly due to a lag in the development of wisdom (**Hochma**) and/or empathy and compassion (**Hesed**). Perhaps we can see Eric Harris, Lionel Tate and their actions at Columbine High School in this light. They and other perpetrators of school shootings are driven by such emotions as anger, humiliation and inadequacy (**Hod**). They then gain access to guns (**Gevurah**). Unfortunately, they experience an immature development in **Hochma, Hesed** and **Netsach** that enables their emotions to rule.

The Holocaust and bin Laden Terrorism

Perhaps now, we can further understand the source of the evil of Hitler. Given intelligence to carry out, the power to do it, and the emotional drive, you have a Hitler. Hitler represents the extreme of **Binah, Gevurah** and **Hod**, the forces of the left side, the *sitra ochra*, with no tempering and balancing from the right, the forces of **Hochma, Hesed** and **Netsach**. Hitler and his henchmen were driven by the emotions of prejudice, hatred, resentment, shame, humiliation; a need to hold and exert power; an intelligence enabling conversion of technology to goals of conquest, subordination and genocide.

From the right side, the perpetrators of the holocaust had tunnel vision. They could not see the foolishness and irrationality of their thinking from lack of **Hochma**. The Nazis lacked any capacity for empathy for their victims from absence of **Hesed**. They could not feel the pain of their victims and had no regard for the sanctity of life. Finally, Nazi "mission" and how it was carried out represents the deepest corruption of our ability to receive values and purpose from heaven due to a blockage of **Netsach**. Ultimately, raw **Binah**, and unmitigated **Gevurah,** combined with the negative motivational emotions of **Hod,** led to the murder of 6 million Jews and 3 million others and a horrible world war to stop him.

Did God allow the holocaust? Now, we can see why this is an irrelevant question. Understood through Kabbalah, evil is a necessary potentiality for there to be ongoing creation. Free will, freedom to be a creating partner with God, cannot exist without the potentiality for and danger of an out of balance left side. God cried with the Jewish people and the world, but God gave us the drive, fortitude, disgust, anger, principles, power, kindness, understanding, and wisdom to defeat evil in the embodiment of the Nazis.

Today, still, evil reappears. It manifests in the acts of Saddam Hussein, Osama bin Laden, Mafiosi, and other emotionally driven, self-centered, foolish tyrants of the left side. Bin Laden and the terrorists who carry out his evil, so clearly represent dominance of the left side and void on the right. Without **Hochma** and **Binah,** they cannot seem to see the complete picture. Their understanding lacks wisdom, compassion or values. Through **Hochma,** we can see that the al Qaeda worldview is warped and simplistic, their actions futile, their understanding superficial. Yet they understand how to create bombs, plan complex hijackings and deliver biological terror.

In terms of **Hesed** and **Gevurah/Din** the al Qaeda terrorists have lost the capacity for feeling the pain of their victims. But, together they have power, the power of **Din**. They surely build on each other's commitment and as a group have far greater potential for destruction than any acting in isolation. With bin Laden's financing, they can muster the **Gevurah** to carry out their plans. The international network of terrorist cells gives them the support and connections, the **Din**, to carry out their warped mission.

Not unlike Hitler, bin Laden's values are emotion driven, certainly not received from above (as he devoutly believes). Lacking the ability to receive divine inspired mission, values, and ethics and to derive holy principles and law, he may believe his mission is holy, but clearly it is the opposite. Rather, his probable motivation is hatred, anger, jealousy, resentment and the pleasures derived from self-esteem, dominance, and power. The manifestations of **Hod** dominate the **Hod – Netsach** continuum for Osama bin Laden.

But, although God creates a world in which Hitler, Hussein and bin Laden can manifest their personal potentialities for evil, humanity also receives the gifts of the right side: the values, compassion and wisdom to combat the forces of evil. People worldwide have experienced intense emotional motivation from September 11. Humanity has the power and leadership. We have the intelligence. But, from the right side, we also have the wisdom, the compassion for other human beings, and the God given values and sense of mission to defeat bin Laden and al Qaeda.

As mentioned in the last chapter, Passover celebrates the power of the left side as Jews drink the symbol of **Gevurah**, wine, leaning to the left. This is truly why this night is different from all other nights. But Passover also teaches to stimulate the power of the right side. It teaches about holiness through restoring balance to defeat the evil inclination embodied by isolated left side forces. Moses may have gravely sinned in slaughtering the Midianites; but Moses is also the law giver, the value and principle maker. Together, the value-based motivating power of **Netsach** and the emotional motivating power of **Hod**, in balance, enable us to defeat evil stemming from such intense emotions as hate, envy and vengeance in the extreme.

At each level in the realm of the Sefirot there is potential for loss of equilibrium resulting in sin and evil. But, there are also forces harmonizing and balancing the Sefirot. In Chapter IV, we explore these balancing forces.

Chapter IV

The Central Column - Balance and Holiness

In the 16th century, Moses Cordovera wrote:

Extremes appear in three places, each of which includes a balance. The first polarity is between Netsach and Hod, and the harmonizer is Yesod. The second polarity is Hesed and Gevurah, and the harmonizer is Tiferet. The third polarity is Hochma and Binah, and the harmonizer is Tiferet in the Mystery of Da'at. Such harmonization entails mediating between the two extremes.[7]

In the center, balancing and harmonizing the Tree of Life (Figure 1, Page 17, 109) are the Sefirot of

Keter,

(Da'at),

Tiferet,

Yesod,

Malchut.

Without the balancing and mediating effect of the central pillar, we have an unholy world. In fact, holiness is an alternate name for **Tiferet**. Righteousness is an alternate name for **Yesod**. The Shechinah (the presence of God) is an alternate name for **Malchut**. King (the ultimate ruler of creation) is an alternate names for **Keter**.

In prayer, when speaking of *holiness*, or of *The Holy One Blessed Be He*, or simply of *Yod Heh Vav Heh* (the holy name of

---

[7]Moses Cordovero, *Or Ne'erav*, 16th century as translated by Daniel C. Matt in *The Essential Kabbalah*, Harper San Francisco, 1995, p. 46.

God), the Kabbalists think **Tiferet**. The holiness of God balances and mediates the Sefirot. It is the nucleus of the orbiting and dynamic Sefirotic realms. It represents the capacity within us for holiness. Such holiness, such true closeness to God, is perfect balance, perfect harmony, perfect equilibrium, in ourselves, our lives, our creation.

Tiferet represents moral equilibrium. It represents an equilibrium between **Hesed** and **Gevurah**. It gives us the power of moral judgment and decision. It bestows on us responsibility for sin.

"Sin," in Hebrew, is *het,* which also means a **"miss."** In Judaism, sin thus has the connotation of "missing the mark," i.e., becoming out of balance. If we fall out of centerline balance, we sin. "Repentance" in Hebrew is *Teshuvah*, related to the word **return**. Thus, as we repent we return ourselves to the centerline, to the balance/equilibrium of **Tiferet**.

Tiferet, by some Kabbalists, is also called *emet,* truth, for truth is in its essence honesty in seeing right from wrong and in recognizing holiness in balance. **Tiferet** represents recognition and awareness of truth when we see it. **Tiferet** represents our yearning for truth and perfection and repentance.

Yesod is positioned centrally directly below **Tiferet**. It represents foundation and grounded ness in our own lives and within ourselves. It represents our ability to be aware of, to feel and to know our needs.

The Kabbalists' association of **Yesod** with *tzedek,* righteousness, is apropos. Righteousness is the ability to live a perfectly need-balanced life. It represents balance in all our relationships, control of our emotions, and ascendancy of good values. A righteous person, a *tsadik*, lives a life exemplifying the values and principles of highest regard to our community. He/she demonstrates perfect harmony between **Netsach** and **Hod**. This is grounded ness. This is perfect dominance over and balance of one's needs.

In Hassidism, the *tsadik* is more than a rabbi. The *tsadik* represents perfection in life, a true leader as exemplar of and teacher of the highest principles, the truest values. The *tsadik* stands between and mediates between the holiness of God, **Tiferet,** and our ability to experience and receive God, the Shechinah/**Malchut.** As depicted in the traditional "Tree of Life" diagram (Figure 1, page 17, 109), **Yesod,** the Sefirah associated with righteousness, is located in the central column directly between **Tiferet** and **Malchut.**

> *"The righteous are the foundation (Yesod) of the world"*
> *Proverbs* 10:25

Our ability to receive the spirituality of God, to *experience* God, is also part of the central column. In Judaism the name of God referring to the indwelling sense of God among us is called the Shechinah. To the Kabbalist the Shechinah is **Malchut.** The Shechinah (**Malchut**) is balanced, harmonious receptivity to God. The Shechinah is thus defined as a "female" Sefirah. Through Her, we can receive spirituality; we receive the potential for balanced co-creation partnering; we birth holy actions in the world.

Through the Shechinah, we receive the holiness of God and become holy ourselves. **Tiferet,** the source of holiness, is a male Sefirah. The sperm of **Tiferet** can impregnate us in **Malchut** through the motivating drives of **Yesod** and enable the birth of ideas, concepts, discoveries, artistic expression and children. Human beings can feel holy and become holy in receiving this wondrous flow of holiness from YHVH, **Tiferet.**

The service welcoming the Sabbath on Friday evening, the Kabbalat Shabbat service, developed by Isaac Luria and his disciples in Tsevat in the 16th century, enlivens and spiritualizes this Kabbalistic concept of holiness. We can welcome the Sabbath and the Sabbath bride (the Shechinah), make the Sabbath holy, and in the process make ourselves holy.

The Lecha Dodi prayer is the cornerstone of the Kabbalat Shabbat service, yet, is understood by few. It is a wondrous poem about the marriage (Kiddushin), or making holy, of **Tiferet** and **Malchut.** The Hebrew word for marriage is the same for consecration or making holy. Every Sabbath eve is a renewal marriage of YHVH and the Shechinah, the son and daughter among the Sefirot, the sun and moon, the male (seed) and female (womb).

We sing, "*Lecha dodi likrat kala, p'nai shabbat nikabalah*" - *To you, my beloved, called a bride, the openings/faces/countenances of Sabbath we can receive.*

On the Sabbath, we can receive holiness; we can become holy; we can restore balance in our lives. We rest from creation partnering and assess our progress in our own personal creation mission.

Chapter V

Understanding Sin - Awareness of Balance

The centerline is not only the pillar of balance. It is also the column of awareness. At each level a form of awareness impacts on our tendency for and responsibility for sin.

Keter - State of One-ness with Ayn Sof, Devekut

Da'at - Knowledge Awareness, Memory, Learning Awareness

Tiferet - Right and Wrong Awareness

Yesod - Need Awareness

Malchut - God Awareness, Experiencing of God's Presence

As mentioned in the previous chapter, the Hebrew word for sin, *het*, literally means a "miss." Missing the mark connotes awareness of a goal or objective and awareness that you came up short. At each level (World - Olam) of the Sefirot, this sense of missing the target manifests differently.

Level I - Asiyah

In the level of Asiyah, **Malchut** represents awareness of God. We sin when we lose, perhaps even for a moment, our God-consciousness. When we forget our divine connection, we lose the sense of presence of the Shechinah. We may become self-focused, self-engrossed, self-centered. By staying God-centered, we can avoid the enticement of sin. In the course of day-to-day living even the most pious of us may become distracted. For a moment we forget God, focusing instead on our own needs and wants.

The observant, traditional Jew is constantly reminded of God's presence throughout the day: in performing *mitzvot* (commandments*)*, before eating, on rising, on retiring for the night, in keeping Kosher. Observing the dietary laws not only reminds the observant Jew constantly of God's nearness, but also encourages one to think about everything that goes into his/her mouth. The week is structured in holy and non-holy time; the Shabbat represents a making holy of time through a heightened awareness of the Shechinah, of God's presence.

In terms of "sin," the observant Jew might feel a need to repent whenever he or she forgets God by forgetting a commandment. A mistake in keeping Kosher, inadvertently violating Sabbath observance, missing an opportunity for a blessing might be construed as "sin" to one who structures one's entire daily life around awareness of the Shechinah.

Analyzing **Malchut** sin on another plane, a loss of **Malchut**-awareness might mean forgetting in our speech or actions the holiness of another human being; hurting another by a thoughtless, emotion-driven act. We often feel sorry later, when we come to recognize that we "lost it for a moment." This, again, is an example of losing **Malchut** balance, losing our sense of God's continuous presence by losing awareness of the holiness of others and, thus, becoming susceptible to sin. Sin here becomes defined as an act or word that we feel sorry for later, that we regret having said or done.

God, through **Malchut**, gives us this sense of *other awareness*, I-thou, that enables us to recognize our mistakes and to strive to stay balanced and God-aware every moment and in every action.

Level II - Yetzirah

In the level of Yetzirah, **Yesod** represents need-awareness. We all have needs. God gives us the ability to <u>know</u> our needs as well as <u>feel</u> our needs. If we just feel needs, we are likely to satisfy the felt need from **Gevurah, Binah** and **Hod**, from the left side. Yesod-balance connotes conscious awareness that we have a need. Awareness opens the opportunity for the felt-need coming from the left to become tempered by, and balanced through **Netsach** on the right. Our values and the principles and laws derived from them, need attention and focus to take hold. God thus gives us **Yesod** as a foundation for need-awareness, as an opportunity to balance the emotions God endows to motivate us to satisfy our needs and to survive and grow, with God instilled values.

When we're hungry and we grab or hoard food when others are hungry, we sin. Our selfishness feeds only our own need, our own hunger. If we lose or ignore such values as sharing, helping others, working together, feeding the helpless; there is nothing to inhibit impulsive acts out of raw, animalistic drives, instincts, hunger and pain.

As we all know, our sexual drives provide powerful impetuses for sinful acts. From the left side we feel love and protectiveness, but also we experience jealousy, insecurity, and rejection. From the right, these emotions are tempered by our awareness of guiding principles, derived from an awareness of our God-connected values.

The institution of marriage is the embodiment of our principles, norms and values with respect to family, responsibility and sexual restraint. Marriage in Judaism is a making holy (a Kiddushin). This making holy, Kabbalistically speaking, is the establishment of a foundation for achieving and maintaining the balance between our sexual drives and needs and our principles and values.

Values and principles can only influence our actions if we recognize our need and make ourselves aware of our values and principles. If we lack values, we truly do become animals; we sin. At times we are tempted to react, strike out, or act impulsively. But our values and principles help guard against this *yetzir ha rah*, this evil inclination. **Yesod** gives us awareness of both our emotions and our values and thus the ability to balance them for balanced, ethical motivation.

Level III - Beriah

Tiferet, on the level of Beriah, represents right/wrong awareness. In biting the apple from the tree of knowledge of right and wrong, Adam and Eve evolved from basic need awareness to sin and ethics awareness. We have responsibility to balance **Gevurah** and **Hesed**. We have responsibility to arouse and recognize our values from **Netsach** and merge them into our emotions from **Hod**. We have responsibility to cultivate our compassion from **Hesed** and merge it into our power to act from **Gevurah**.

If we fail, if we sin, our conscience informs us. The holiness of God, through **Tiferet**, enables us to recognize when we "miss the mark" and to atone.

On Yom Kippur, the Jewish people recognize not only their own individual sins, but the sins of the entire congregation, the entire Jewish people and the entire world. On this day, God gives us the opportunity to lean to the right. We pray for God's **Hesed** to balance and preside over God's **Din/Gevurah**. We also pray for God's **Gevurah/Din** and **Hesed** to balance within ourselves.

This can only happen if we become actively aware of our sins and proactively strengthen our sense of **Hesed** with the goal of undoing the wrong. We can only atone if we recognize the sin, undo the wrong and vow that if given the opportunity or circumstance again, we would *not* sin.

This is **Tiferet**-consciousness. When we atone and are forgiven, we achieve a form of holiness.

Level IV - Atzilut

In the world of Atzilut, the confluence of **Hochma** and **Binah** are represented in **Da'at** and the highest-most source, **Keter**. **Da'at** (knowledge), itself, is not defined as a Sefirah. It, itself, is not a force for co-creation. Rather, it is a result, a manifestation. It is the combination of wisdom and understanding as knowledge.

Da'at thus represents *knowledge-awareness* in our hierarchy of balance and sin. Knowledge-awareness is memory. When we know we have sinned, when we know it was wrong, when we remember the effects and yet when we do it again, we commit the highest level of sin. We have ignored God, ignored our values, buried our sense of goodness, and subdued our conscience. We have tapped our understanding (**Binah**) without wisdom (**Hochma**). We have committed true evil.

Memory is a marvelous gift from God. It enables us to learn and thus to create. It also enables us to grow morally. We can remember, through our wisdom and understanding, the effects of our actions; we can remember and learn from our mistakes; we can remember the suffering we caused and remember how we felt; we can remember not to do it again. We can also remember the mistakes and sins of others and how we felt as the victim of another's sin.

Memory and knowledge also brings responsibility. When we remember suffering and become aware of imperfection in the world, we hold a responsibility to act, to correct, to restore. This is Tikun Olam, fixing of the world. **Da'at**-consciousness enables us to recognize problems, perceive opportunities to improve society, identify needs for new laws, organizations or structures. We then have responsibility as Jews and as moral individuals to act. Not to act is to sin; not to act violates the balance of **Da'at**-holiness.

Level V - Devekut

The highest level of awareness is conceptualized in the Kabbalah as *Devekut*: Connective ness. **Keter**-consciousness is like achieving a oneness with God, the unknowable source. **Keter** oneness is total unity beyond the capacity to sin. The Kabbalists call this utmost communion with God, this total perfection, *Devekut*.

Only the holiest individual could possibly attain *Devekut*; perhaps it is only a goal; perhaps, no one could truly achieve **Keter**-awareness. But, perhaps it is the goal that *het*, sin, keeps us from achieving. Missing the mark, perhaps, is really a form of falling further away from our ultimate objective, reaching the source, reaching full and true balance, reaching **Keter** unity, *Devekut*.

In the next chapter we explore how the Kabbalah can guide us not only in understanding evil and sin, but also in assessing ethics.

Chapter VI
A Guide to Ethics

The challenge, now that I've presented a Kabbalistic understanding of evil and sin, is to apply the Kabbalah tradition toward developing a framework for contemporary Jewish ethics. Ethics is what guides our sense of propriety in day-to-day life. Our sense of ethics guides us in interpersonal relationships, business activities, legal and political issues, professional conduct and family dynamics.

From Aristotle to Kant to Schopenhauer, philosophers have debated categorical imperatives, natural right or wrong, and the nature of evil. Today, lively debate continues in the legal profession, within the business community, among theologians, in politics, at schools and in our homes. Can we develop a guide for ethical behavior? Is there a universal guide to help us make the right choices? Is there a framework for assessing others actions as well as our own, and to learn from our mistakes?

In this book, we start from an understanding that God is the source for the urge for centeredness, the phenomenon of balance, homeostasis as a force returning us to equilibrium. As Kabbalah teaches, our natural desire to help others, to be altruistic, to feel compassion is a flow from God that we call **Hesed**. The values and derived principles that guide our sense of right, wrong and ethics also source in the unknowable God. This cognitive awareness of ethics is **Netsach**. The ability for abstract conceptualization that can take these values defining "right"(**Netsach**) and this yearning to help others (**Hesed**) and develop ideas, theories and thought, the Kabbalah terms **Hochma**.

Out of our **Hochma**, **Netsach** and **Hesed** comes a sense of purpose to our lives that the Kabbalah calls Tikun Olam. As elaborated in Chapter 1, Tikun Olam represents our partnership with God in ongoing creation to "fix the world," working toward perfection and a Messianic age. Personally, on a private level, and socially, on a communal, Jewish peoplehood and national level, we accomplish Tikun Olam. We may not recognize our personal mission, but perhaps it is the justification for receiving the glorious Sefirot from The Source. Our conscious receptivity to our purpose and role in life is an aspect of **Netsach**. **Netsach** is the seat of ethics in that it represents our very ability to devise and understand the values and principles that guide our actions.

Ethics is a framework for helping us to define ourselves as good human beings and good Jews. It guides our choices as we strive to "do the right thing" in a given situation or dilemma. Ethics is an intercourse of **Hochma** into **Hesed** into **Netsach**. When **Hesed** flows into **Netsach** we feel a positive glow to our values; we feel the desire to help others; our goals become altruistic. When **Hochma** flows into **Hesed** and **Netsach,** we inject an element of humanity and intelligence into our choices and decisions.

In the preceding chapters we have explored how evil results when the left side dominates the right. Through Kabbalah, we understand sin in terms of loss of balance and equilibrium in the Sefirotic dynamic. Ethics, on the other hand, is primarily a right side phenomenon.

The right side is the seat of ethics. If any one of the three forces of the right become blocked, curtailed or limited, resulting actions could be construed as "unethical." In this sense, Kabbalah provides a powerful framework to guide our current behavior and choices and to assess past actions and decisions.

At the level of Yitzirah

In Yetzirah, ethical questions can be assessed in terms of shortfall in **Netsach**. **Netsach**, as the origin of our values and principles, represents our cognitive recognition of ethics. Our natural sense of values and our ability to teach and share values is a common understanding of "ethics".

A shortfall in **Netsach** results by definition in an act that is "unprincipled" or counter to our understood values. Often our values and principles tell us to do one thing but our emotions motivate us to do the other.

At the level of Yetzirah values temper and direct emotions. As the *Zohar* teaches, anger in isolation is *yetzir ha rah*, the force of evil inclination. But, if balanced with **Netsach**, it is an essential motivational gift. Raw isolated anger leads directly to immorality and unethical behavior in law, business or human relations, but anger, constrained by values and principles is what motivates us to respond to injustice and unfairness.

In *Torah*, Jacob violates principles of fairness and honesty in his dealings with Laban, as perhaps Laban does with Jacob. Noah violates the love and respect for his son, and in his anger curses Ham's son Canaan, an apparently innocent bystander. Abraham experiences a shortfall in **Netsach** in his treatment of Hagar and in nearly sacrificing Isaac before the "fullness of YHVH" brings him back into balance.

Both Abraham and Isaac told foreign rulers that their wives were their sisters, violating concepts of truthfulness and endangering their wives.

Shimon and Levy's impulsive anger-driven and lawless response to Dina's rape in slaughtering all the Hivite males was clearly a lapse in **Netsach**; and all the brothers' lynch mob action in plundering the town represents a dramatic lawlessness.

In modern life, examples of **Netsach** shortfall might include any intentional and cognitive violation of our values. If we knowingly perform an act or make a decision we know is "wrong," we are clearly acting unethically. Does it really matter if "no one was hurt" or "no one knew?" We know if we cheated, if we broke the law, if we violated the commandments.

Here are some examples of **Netsach** shortfalls that might be defined as unethical even without compounding shortfalls in **Hesed** or **Hochma**:

- If, for example, chief executive and financial officers of a publicly traded company employ aggressive or creative accounting to mislead investors as to true performance, they are violating values of honesty and integrity.

- A Princeton University admissions officer hacks into the security protected Web site of Yale admissions. Even if no one is hurt by the action, even if it is not unwise, it is a violation of the fundamental principles of academic honesty universities ingrain upon both students and faculty.

At the Level of Beriah

A shortfall in **Hesed** we call selfishness. Self-centeredness/ egoism is the contrary of **Hesed**.

If the result of our selfishness is harm to another, then we have violated **Hesed**-ethics. Acts that in any way hurt another could be seen as shortfalls in **Hesed**, shortfalls in our innate sense of care for one another.

Jacob in stealing the birthright of Esau is committing a selfish act.

Laban, in his dealings with Jacob, acts for his own selfish interests at the expense of Jacob and his daughters.

Rachel in stealing Laban's idols acted not just foolishly, it was selfishly.

In a direct act of **Hesed**, a symbol of **Hesed**, providing water for the thirsty, Moses commits a self-centered act by demonstrably hitting the rock and claiming personal credit for God's **Hesed**. Moses' shortfall in **Hesed** is at the expense of YHVH.

The manifestation of **Hesed** shortfall, i.e. self-centeredness that costs or harms another, is common in contemporary life:

- The attorney who is more concerned with his own interests than his clients may overcharge, or unnecessarily extent or delay the case.

- The business marketer who for profit maximization creates costs to others may engage in telemarketing or spamming to make sales. The marketer is selfishly disturbing others to sell his product.

- A drug company may strategically choose to limit production and distribution of a life saving pharmaceutical to maximize near term profits.

- The doctor who is more concerned about reputation, peer esteem or earnings than the welfare of her patients

At the Level of Atzilut

Sefer Yitzirah states, *"Tumerat Hochma iveret" (IV: 13).* The contrast or antithesis of **Hochma** is foolishness. If we lose the flow of **Hochma**, even for a moment, we could make a foolish or "stupid" decision. We might say something we regret later. We might act "unethically." Foolishness is acting without thinking. It is acting without fully utilizing our God-given abilities to reason, analyze, interpret, and conceptualize.

Not being as wise as we are capable, curtailed **Hochma**, results in actions or decisions that may not be "sinful" but may nevertheless be of questionable ethics. In essence, we could have done better, but we didn't. Not just foolishness, but also carelessness, could result from a shortfall in **Hochma**.

Abraham reasoned with YHVH (**Tiferet**) over the destruction of Sodom and Gomorrah. Abraham argued,

Perhaps there are 50 righteous within the city; would you sweep away and not forgive the place on account of the 50 righteous that are near it." **Genesis**18 (24)

God agrees with Abraham's wisdom, if there are 50 righteous men God would not destroy the cities. Abraham continues the argument down to 10 righteous men and God continues to agree. But then Abraham stops. Why doesn't he continue to one righteous person, Lot, and save the cities? His wisdom seems to abate at 10. He gives up.

Isaac suffers a curtailment of wisdom in bestowing his blessing on Jacob rather than Esau. Perhaps he is "fooled," but foolishness is allowing oneself to be "fooled." The blind Isaac perhaps had lost his **Hochma**.

Torah seems to be saying that the secret departure of Jacob from Laban was unethical in stating, *"Jacob stole the heart of Laban in not telling him that he was fleeing."* (**Genesis**31 (20)) In the

Hebrew, he stole the *lev* (heart) of *Levan* (Laban) in the foolish and unnecessary act of departing without the proper farewell.

Later, Jacob clearly and demonstrably favors Joseph over his brothers. Again, such favoritism by a parent is both unwise and foolish. In contrast is Joseph's treatment of his brothers in Egypt. He displays fullest wisdom in reuniting and restoring family unity. He demonstrates patients, thoughtfulness, strategy and foresight in staging an opportunity for repentance and righting by the brothers.

The **Genesis** story of creation teaches that with the gift of capability for wisdom comes responsibility for acting wisely. Analysis of **Hochma** ethics can be a guide for our decisions.

In contemporary life, here are common instances of curtailed **Hochma:**

- A lawyer does not use his fullest and utmost abilities and energies in defense of his client.

- A doctor does not explore all the options and thus misdiagnoses. In the sense of **Hochma** ethics, professional malpractice could be construed as a breach of ethics.

- A business executive becomes lazy and careless; his poor decisions cost his employees their jobs and his investors their money.

- A scientist conducts dangerous research without fully considering the risks and wider implications.

Actions that represent shortfalls in multiple right side Sefirot become truly unethical. The perpetrator of a foolish act, by say reckless driving that puts himself in danger, may be simply foolish, not unethical. But, if combined with selfishly endangering passengers in the car or in other vehicles on the road, he is committing an act that is not just foolish but also selfishly endangers others and violates fundamental values of preserving the safety of others and obeying the law. Such an act represents a shortfall in Hochma, Hesed **and** Netsach.

In the next part of *Understanding Evil,* we explore how *Torah* can shed light on this Kabbalistic approach to evil, sin and ethics.

Chapter VII

The Origins of Evil - The Story of Cain and Abel

Genesis is the story of God's creation and humankind's capacity to co-create. To understand why and how God created evil, let's explore the mysterious story of *Cain and Abel*.

This story raises major questions. Why did God allow Cain to murder Abel? Why does God seem to favor Abel's offering while not noticing Cain's? What is the meaning of Cain's emotional reaction? How do we read the implied scoff of "Am I my brother's keeper?" Why does God create a sign to protect Cain after his sin?

The story comes together beautifully if you understand the hidden Kabbalistic meaning. *Cain and Abel* is about the creation/evolution of the left side - **Hod, Gevurah** and **Binah** and the origin of the potentiality for sin. Here's my literal translation:

> *And Adam knew Eve, his woman, and she conceived and gave birth to Cain. She said, "I acquired a man, from YHVH." She added to this and gave birth to his brother, Abel.*
>
> *It came to be that Abel became a shepherd and Cain was a worker of the ground. It came to be after time, Cain brought an offering for YHVH from the fruit of the ground. Also Abel brought from the first born of his sheep and of its fat. YHVH noticed Abel and his offering. And to Cain and to his offering, he did not notice. Cain got very angry and his face fell. YHVH said to Cain, "Why are you angry and why did your face fall? Listen, if you make good, it will be lifted up. And if you do not make good, the opening for sin lies waiting. And to you is its desire. And you will be the ruler of it."*
>
> *Cain said something to Abel his brother. And it came to be when they were in the field, Cain rose up to Abel his brother and killed him. YHVH said to Cain "Where is Abel your*

brother?" He said, "I did not know I am the guard of my brother." He said, "What did you do? The voice of the blood of your brother yells to me from the ground. And now you are cursed from the ground that opened her mouth to take the blood of your brother from your hand. For you will work the ground. No longer will it give her strength. You will be a fugitive and a wanderer across the land." Cain said to YHVH, " My burden is greater than I can carry. Behold, you have banished me today from on the face of the ground. And from your face I will be hidden. I will be a fugitive and a wanderer in the land and it will be that all that find me will kill me." YHVH said to him, "Therefore, any who kill Cain, sevenfold vengeance shall be taken." YHVH placed a sign for Cain for all that find him not to hurt him. Cain left from before YHVH and lived in the land of Nod before Eden.

Understanding this story as a continuation of the creation story, yields a revealing Kabbalistic interpretation about the creation of the Sefirot.

The Torah tells us that Cain works the land. He invented farming. Cain also is the first human being to display and act from emotion. Finally, he is the first to exert power through strength over another human being. Cain thus represents the evolution of **Binah**, **Hod** and **Gevurah/Din**. He is the first human being with the power of the left side, the ability to receive these Sefirot from Ayn Sof.

Abel, in contrast, does not even have a speaking part. Abel is a passive being, a shepherd of sheep. He does not demonstrate the ability or the strength or the desire to control his environment and shape it to survive.

YHVH, the **Tiferet** code name, the balancing and modulating force, *notices* (recognizes the balance in) the passive shepherd, Abel. But YHVH is tacit with respect to Cain and his "new technology" of agriculture. Recognizing the potentiality of evil and sin from left side dominance, YHVH acutely warns Cain, " *And if you do not make good, the opening for sin lies waiting. And to you is its desire. And you will be the ruler of it."* In other words, if you do not make goodness out of the powers I have given you through the Sefirot, the potential for sin lies waiting. You will experience its (sin's) desire, its pull. And you will be the ruler (controller) of it; you have power over it.

Cain has received from God the formidable powers of the left column: intelligence to grow food and farm; the capacity to build agriculturally based communities and civilizations; and emotional motivation as the fuel to work the land.

Yet with these wondrous forces comes sin couching at the door. The enticement of it will always be there. But you, Cain, have the free will to balance the forces of the left and not to let your emotions (your face falling) fuel sin. You, as the ruler of sin's desire, will be given responsibility for morality and sin.

But Cain lacks the wisdom, compassion and values of the right side. **Hochma, Hesed** and **Netsach** are still evolving. The result is an act God cannot control, cannot stop without terminating **Binah, Gevurah** and **Hod** as forces, just as God could not stop the process and result of the holocaust.

YHVH asks, "Where's Abel." Cain gives with the mysterious response, *"I did not know I am the guardian of my brother."* He is not expressing scorn or lack of care, as erroneously implied in the alternate translation, *"I don't know. Am I my brother's keeper?"* Rather, Cain is like a child. He has not yet grown and evolved to know he is responsible for his brother, to know there are natural principles by which we live.

Learning to be the guardian of one's brother is the birth of **Netsach**, our capacity to receive and internalize fundamental principles and values. Humankind is evolving a capacity to balance and control our emotions, a capacity to balance the satisfaction of our innate needs. This balance is achieved through values, provided through the force of **Netsach**. We learn the value of responsibility for our brother, that we are our brothers' guardians.

In the light of the situation, YHVH's treatment of Cain exemplifies the ethical. The solution is with wisdom, kindness and principle (**Hochma, Hesed and Netsach**). God separates Cain by exiling him. God puts a sign on him, now that he knows death and fear, to protect him from the animals. In essence, God's protecting sign and proclamation are a first principle, a beginning for **Netsach**.

78

God's treatment of Cain, a being with powers of the left side but not the right, is separation and isolation, so he cannot destroy through his powers.

Generations later, Noah is endowed with **Binah**, **Gevurah** and **Hod** in sufficient balance with **Hochma**, **Hesed** and **Netsach** to save humankind and all life. He is able to overcome and survive natural disaster. Man is evolving toward becoming a more balanced creation partner with God.

Chapter VIII

The Ability to Satisfy Our Needs - Noah and the Forces of Nature

In the *Genesis* story of creation, Noah represents the evolution of need awareness. Noah becomes a partner with God (Elohim) in creating solutions for survival. Following is my literal translation of the introduction of the Noah story:

Genesis VI: 9-22.

These are the generations of Noah, Noah, a righteous man, wholehearted he was in his time. Noah moved himself forth for Ha Elohim. Noah begot three sons, Shem, Ham, and Yapheth. The earth was slaughtering before Ha Elohim. The earth was filled with violence. Elohim saw[8] the earth. Behold it was slaughtering, for all meat had slaughtered its way on the earth.

Elohim said to Noah, "an end of all meat is coming before me, for the earth is full of corruption from them. And behold, I shall slaughter them, slaughter the earth. Make for yourself an ark of gopher wood. Make the ark with rooms. Pitch it inside and out. And this is how you will make it: three hundred cubits length of the ark, fifty cubits width of it, thirty cubits height of it. You will make a skylight for the ark and God (El)[9]. You will complete it a cubit from above. And you will put an opening of the ark in its side. You will make lower, second and third levels. And I, here myself, bring a flood of water on the earth to slaughter all meat that within it has the soul (ruach) of life. From under the sky all that is in earth shall perish. I shall establish with you my covenant. You will come to the ark, you and your sons and your wife

---

[8] Closely related to the word for "fear."

[9] El is the name for God associated with **Hesed.**

and the women of your sons with you. And from all living from all meat, two from all will you bring to the ark to live with you. They will be male and female. From foul from their type, from beasts from their type, from earth creepers from their type, two from all you will bring to you to live. And you take for yourself from all foods that you will eat and gather for yourself and it will be for you and for them for eating." Noah did according to all that Elohim commanded, yes he did.

Elohim, the name of God associated with **Gevurah** and hence with natural disaster, gives precise instructions for a creation that will save creation. God does not build the ark for Noah; Noah does not create the ark independently. It is a partnership. Each needs the other to conceive, design and construct the ark.

Elohim is precise not only on how to build the ark, but also about what will happen and the purpose of the ark. Elohim sees all meat as slaughtering each other for survival. The plan had gone awry. No longer was there perfection and balance. Noah's task is to assist Elohim (the power side of God, not YHVH, the balance restoring aspect of God) to preserve each form of life from the natural disaster that is coming.

Noah is called " *a righteous man, wholehearted he was in his time.*" Noah was righteous in his generation. He was simple, wholehearted. In Kabbalistic writings, "righteousness" (*tzedek*) is a code name for **Yesod**. Simple and wholehearted similarly allude to **Yesod**.

Awareness of our fundamental needs and the ability to satisfy those needs are God-given capabilities. They enable our survival, growth and creativity. As explained in Chapter II, the Sefirah of **Yesod** represents our survival drives and instincts and awareness of our needs so that we can satisfy them.

In the story of creation, in "*moving himself forth for HaElohim,*" Noah becomes the first human being to recognize his needs and those of the animals in his care. He becomes the first being to use his God-given abilities to overcome natural disaster, take control over nature and control his own destiny. Noah, facing the

81

flood, is able to partner with Elohim (God's power) to enable learning and invention. Noah learns how to make a boat and how to save himself, his family and the diversity of animal life.

Noah also represents the evolution of **Binah** (understanding), our ability to invent and solve. Directions to build come from Elohim. As communicated in the Noah story, **Binah** is the manifestation of our ability to understand our environment and to create the technology to assure we can survive the forces of nature.

God's rainbow covenant assures us that through **Binah** man will always be capable of overcoming nature. We'll learn to build shelter, to predict hurricanes, to protect ourselves from wild arrivals, to fight and cure disease, to control famine, and to survive earthquakes, tidal waves, forest fires, volcanoes and tornadoes. Symbolically speaking, Noah represents our ability to recognize our needs and to use intelligence and invention to overcome them. As implied in the covenant translated below, humankind will always walk with Elohim; we have the **Gevurah** to overcome natural disaster and shelter ourselves from nature.

When the power forces of Elohim destroys life, only Noah, the righteous and wholehearted, the man of **Yesod** and **Binah**, is endowed with the means for survival.

But, is Elohim, associated with the left side, also recognizing Her own loss of balance? The text stimulates questions about evil, sin and ethics. Was God's act in destroying the world purely an act of Elohim, i.e. of **Gevurah/Din**? Where was **Hochma**? Is there a question of ethics in this "solution" due to the shortfall or even absence of wisdom/**Hochma**? And where was Hesed? Did Elohim lack empathy and love for the beings She is about to destroy?

There is an obscure mention of making a skylight for the ark and El, the God name associated with **Hesed**. Is Elohim making space for **Hesed**, bringing in the light of **Hesed**? Is Elohim planning a role for **Hesed** in the new order? Is the absence of **Hesed** in the world the key problem Elohim is trying to correct? And where is **Netsach**, God's values, in this radical solution?

As translated below, Ha Elohim's statements appear to sound like repentance. Elohim recognizes the sin, expressed sorrow and covenants never again to commit such a sin, such evil.

Genesis IX: 17 - 27

"This is the sign of the covenant that I give between me and you and all living souls that is with you for generations forever. I gave you my rainbow in the cloud. It will be a sign of a covenant between me and the earth. And it will be, when I make clouds over the Earth and the rainbow is seen in the cloud, I shall remember my covenant which is between me and you and all living souls (nefesh)[10] of all flesh. There will not again be the water for a flood to butcher all meat. The rainbow will be in the cloud and I shall see it to remember an everlasting covenant between Elohim and between every living soul (nefesh) in every meat that is on the earth."

The sons of Noah that went out of the ark were Shem, Ham and Yapheth. And Ham is the father of Canaan. These three are the sons of Noah and from these was spread over all the earth.

Noah, a man of the soil, started over. He planted a vineyard. He drank from the wine and became drunk. He was uncovered within his tent. Ham, the father of Canaan, saw the nakedness of his father and told his two brothers outside. Shem and Yapheth took the garment and put it over their shoulders and went forth backwards and did not see the nakedness of their father. The effect of the wine ended for Noah. And he knew what the little son had done to him. He said, "cursed be Canaan. A slave of slaves will he be to his brothers. Bless YHVH, the God of Shem. Let Canaan be their slave. Elohim will make beautiful Yapheth and he shall dwell in the tents of Shem. Let Canaan be a slave to him."

---

[10] Nefesh is the sole associated in Kabbalah with **Yesod** and the World of Yetzirah.

What is the first thing Noah does on surviving the flood and leaving the ark to start over? He plants a vineyard and gets drunk. Here is a wonderful metaphor for becoming out of balance - becoming intoxicated. What is the result? Noah falls asleep naked; he cannot even provide for his most basic needs. His sons must even come in to cover him.

Noah subsequently commits the sin of losing his temper and letting **Hod** overcome his **Yesod** balance. In his anger, he loses touch with his values, **Netsach.** He curses the son of Ham, Canaan, for Ham having "seen the nakedness" of Noah, embarrassing him. In Noah's treatment of Ham and Canaan, where is the **Hochma**? Where is the **Hesed**?

The implication is that Noah's grandson, Canaan, is clearly innocent. Canaan is not even involved. In this story both Noah and God may have been motivated more by frustration and anger than by value, kindness and wisdom. Even Noah, the most righteous and forbearing in his generation, loses his own balance and destroys the cohesiveness of his family, as perhaps Elohim did in destroying with the flood.

I see the covenant and the sign of the rainbow as God's repentance for the evil that nature can wrought. It is a promise to give humankind the ability to restore and maintain harmony and sustain life on earth. Through these Sefirot, God covenants that the forces of nature will never again destroy all living *nefesh*, the Kabbalistic soul associated with Yetzirah. God can sin and God can repent.

The colors of the rainbow symbolize the balanced, harmonized, merged forces of the Sefirot. In the evolution of ongoing creation, humankind is becoming endowed with the potentiality to co-create in partnership with God so that life on this planet can continue to develop. With the help of humankind, life will be preserved and protected, not destroyed.

Today we are increasingly recognizing that the earth is a living organism and we are as cells within this complex macro-organism. The rainbow is a reminder of God's commitment not to destroy our organism by giving humankind the power and mission to preserve, conserve and protect our fragile environment and the precious life it enables.

Chapter IX
Can We Sacrifice Gevurah/Din? - The Binding of Isaac

On the second day of Rosh Hashanah, the *Torah* reading is the story of the binding and near sacrifice of Isaac by Abraham. It's a troubling story for many. On the surface it is about faith. But, particularly on the Day of Remembrance, the story raises troubling questions. What kind of "faith" is God demanding of us? Why does God test Abraham? What is the role of Isaac? Why does an angel stop Abraham?

The Kabbalah sheds insightful light on this controversial story. It's not about faith, although it does deal with testing. But, who is testing whom? Is God testing Abraham, vice versa, or both?

The key to understanding the binding of Isaac story is in the Kabbalistic symbolism connected to names used for God and the forefathers. As explained in the previous chapter on Noah, Ha Elohim is the name of God representing **Gevurah**. Abraham and Isaac approach *Hamakom* (the Place), the spiritual place of God and the Sefirah of **Keter**. YHVH finally speaks through an angel just as Abraham is about to kill off Isaac. YHVH is the personal God we can experience; YHVH represents **Tiferet**, holiness and blessing. It is also crucial to know that to Kabbalists Abraham is code name for **Hesed**; Isaac is a code name for **Gevurah/Din**. Now, read the story with these deciphering keys in mind:

Genesis XXII - The Akada - The Binding of Isaac

> *And it was after these things, Ha Elohim tested Abraham and said to him, "Abraham" and he said, "Here I am." And He said "please take your son, your only that you love, Isaac and go forth to the land of Moriah and offer him there as an offering on one of the mountains that I shall tell you."*

Abraham got up early in the morning. Dressed his donkey. Took two of his youths with him and Isaac his son. He chopped offering wood, got up and walked to the Place that Ha Elohim spoke of. On the third day Abraham lifted his eyes. He saw the Place from afar. Abraham said to his youth "sit here with the donkey and I and the youth will go there. And we'll worship and we'll return to you."

Abraham took the offering wood, put it on Isaac his son, took in his hand the fire and the knife and the two of them went together. Isaac said to Abraham his father, he said "My father" and he said, "Here I am, my son." He said, "Here's the fire and wood and where's the lamb for offering." Abraham said, "Elohim will make appear for himself the offering lamb, my son." They came to the Place that Ha Elohim had told of. Abraham built there an altar. He arranged the wood. He bound Isaac, his son. He put him on the altar, on top of the wood. Abraham sent out his hand; He took the knife to butcher his son.

An angel (your fullness of) YHVH called to him from the heavens. He said, "Abraham, Abraham." He said, "Here I am." He said, "Don't send your hand to the youth. And don't do anything, for now I know that you are an Elohim fearer (Elohim see-er) and you did not withhold your son, your only one, from me." Abraham lifted his eyes and saw (feared). And here is a ram caught in the thicket by his horns. Abraham went and took the ram and offered it instead of his son. Abraham called the name of that place YHVH will be seen, that is said today in the mountain YHVH will be seen.

The angel (fullness) of YHVH called to Abraham a second time from the heavens. He said, "In me I have sworn an oath of YHVH because you have done this thing and not withheld your son, your only one. Because you blessed, I will bless you and through the power of multitude will multiply your seed as the stars of the heavens and as the sand on the shore and your seed will inherit the gate of your enemy. And all the nations of the earth will be blessed through your seed because you heard my voice."

With the Kabbalistic deciphering codes, the story comes alive. The concept of gods, Ha Elohim, also the name associated with **Gevurah/Din**, is the aspect of God that tests Abraham. The angel of YHVH, of **Tiferet**, stops Abraham **(Hesed)** from sacrificing Isaac **(Din/Gevurah)**. YHVH says, "Now I know you are an Elohim Fearer (alternately, an Elohim See-er)." [11]

So appropriate on Rosh Hashanah, the *Torah* reading raises the question of whether our inclination for good can or should try to muzzle, limit, sacrifice the side that brings with it the potential for sin. We fear sin; we fear the left side, the powers of evil. But, if we sacrifice or destroy our **Gevurah**, our **Binah**, our **Hod**, we not only destroy the potentiality for evil, we terminate our very ability to create.

The angel of YHVH, of **Tiferet**, called "Abraham Abraham!" from the heavens. And Abraham hears and becomes aware. **Hesed** cannot eliminate **Din** because **Hesed** alone cannot create. Human beings need **Gevurah, Binah** and **Hod**. We need power, intelligence and motivation to be co-creators.

Understanding **Din** as more than simple power and justice, understanding **Din** as the force that enables coalescence of cells, communities, societies and nations into more and more complex organisms, the Akada has even deeper meaning. Isaac, representing **Din**, is being lead by Abraham - **Hesed**. The coalescence of matter is passive, following the laws of nature, evolving through natural selection, until some force of goodness guides it toward "the Place." When they reach "the Place" (Ha Makom), YHVH presents itself as "the angel of YHVH", through related root, alternatively interpreted, "your fullness of YHVH."

YHVH truly represents the mediating, balancing equilibrium forces of the universe. These forces enable goodness and purpose to interface and interact with the coalescence and development of life and society. Through coalescence, partnering, and community; creation is given new momentum, power, multiplying effect. The

---

[11] The angel could also be seen as a manifestation or messenger of **Netsach,** delivering values to Abraham and his civilization. The value is that of life.

blessing of the angel of YHVH is one of *Veharbah Arbeh*, through the power of making many, I shall give you many seeds, as the stars in heaven, as the sands on the shore. Your seed and your **Din**, Abraham, because they represent the force of **Hesed**, will inherit the gates of your enemies. Enemies here could be interpreted as the potentialities for imbalance, for evil, that are inherent within **Din/Binah/Hod**.

The Binding of Isaac story is thus not about faith, but about our inclination and desire to bind **Gevurah/Din**. In the Cain, Flood and Babel stories there was no **Hesed**. Through Abraham, God introduces **Hesed** as a human force from divine sources. God has created a Sefirah that counters the potential for violence and corruption inherent to Gevurah and Din. At this instance humankind also gains the responsibility for discerning ethics and for acting morally.

The Binding of Isaac is about ongoing creation and the establishment of a force called holiness that enables a balance between left and right. This wondrous holiness is the essence of **Tiferet,** also called YHVH. **Tiferet** is the aspect of God that we can directly experience as a force for homeostasis, whose presence we feel, who makes us holy.

In stopping Abraham (**Hesed**), our fullness of YHVH says, *"For now I know you are an Elohim - Fearer (or Elohim See-er)."* Fearing and seeing Elohim is not about "faith in God." It is about fearing and recognizing **Gevurah**. If we can perceive, recognize and fear the potentiality of **Gevurah**, we can avoid sin, we can achieve and receive **Tiferet.**

The blessing continues: through your seed, Abraham/**Hesed**, will be blessed all the peoples/nations, all the **Din** of the world, following the fact that you received (heard) my voice. Thus, through Abraham, God is creating a special people with a special role. The same blessing is repeated later for Isaac and again for Jacob - through your seed all the nations/**Din** of the world will be blessed. The *Shema Yisroel* - the core blessing of the Jewish faith has special meaning: **"Hear Israel YHVH is our God, YHVH is balance and unity."** Shema means hear, receive, be aware. All the nations, all the **Din**, will be blessed, Abraham, because you *heard* my voice.

Torah through the Binding of Isaac story raises some interesting questions for all of us: In what ways do we sacrifice **Din** in our own lives? And in our societies? Do we face the choices of Abraham? How has **Hesed** effectively limited **Din** in contemporary society through custom, ethics and law? We human beings make choices in controlling, channeling and limiting **Din**

After 9/11, our society questions once again whether we need to constrain free **Gevurah/Din** of the individual. In the age of terrorism does public safety require tradeoffs on our freedoms in order to police the unfettered **Gevurah/Din** of the terrorist? Are these tradeoffs prudent? Are these constraints reflective of our higher values? Can we maintain the perfect balance of **Hesed** and **Gevurah** in fighting terrorism in Israel and worldwide?

We constrain **Gevurah/Din** in limiting the power of government. Democracy by definition limits the authority and power of the state. In contrast, totalitarianism and the evils associated with it, exemplifies unfettered **Din**. But the War on Terrorism and the murderous rein of the suicide bombers in Israel inevitably raise questions on whether we must trade off liberties. Should we be concerned that we not over sacrifice **Din?**

Is there a role for **Hesed** in international affairs? Certainly. It is the force that encourages us to do what feels right, not simply pursue self or sovereign interest. **Hesed** influences us to send troops to Bosnia, Kosovo and East Timor to constrain or defeat the manifestations of tyrannical **Gevurah/Din**. The United States and NATO have chosen to override the sovereign rights of nations who commit genocide against their own people. We prevent holocausts by sacrificing **Din** through the influence and force of **Hesed**.

On the personal, individual level, in our marriages and other interpersonal relationships, we elect to limit **Din**. We bind **Din/Gevurah** in the very recognition that relationships are partnerships. **Hesed** assists us to listen, to hear, to receive and to give in our relationships. Love for spouse, children, parents is a powerful, altruism-enhancing force that limits and binds **Gevurah** and **Din**.

As Abraham and Isaac represent **Hesed** and **Gevurah/Din**, Jacob represents **Tiferet**. In the next chapter we explore messages from the Jacob stories on the creation and strengthening of **Tiferet** within humankind.

Chapter X

Evolution of the Blessing of Tiferet - Jacob, Esau and Israel

(Genesis XXV: 19) –Jacob versus Esau

And these are the generations of Isaac, Abraham's son. Abraham birthed Isaac. Notice Isaac was 40 years old when he took Rivka (Rebecca), Betuel the Aramean's daughter from Paddan Aram, the sister of Laban the Aramean, to himself for a wife. Isaac pleaded to YHVH for the presence of his wife for she was barren. YHVH received his plea and Rivka his wife conceived. The sons struggled within her and she said, "if thus, why am I?" And she went to demand of YHVH. YHVH said to her, "two nations are in your womb and two peoples will be separated from your bowels. And one people from the other people will be stronger and the elder will work for the younger."

And when her time for birth was filled, behold twins are in her womb. And the first came out red all over like a hairy mantle. They called him Esau. And afterward his brother came out and his hand held Esau's heel. They called him Jacob. Isaac was 60 when they were born. The boys grew and Esau was a man knowing hunting, a man of the field. Jacob was a simple man, dwelling in tents.

The theme of the evolution of the *left* and *right* continues in the story of Jacob and his twin brother, Esau. ***These are the generations of Isaac, Abraham's son*** in Kabbalistic code is telling us: these are the offspring of **Gevurah**; this is the evolution of the flows from **Gevurah** to the lower Sefirot. The passage continues, ***Isaac was forty years old when he took Rivka for a wife.*** Forty can be interpreted as a metaphor for rebirth, a reference to forty weeks of pregnancy. (Similarly, the children of Israel wandered forty years in the dessert in birthing a new people).

Isaac, **Gevurah**, is taking a mate, Rivka, the foremother associated with **Netsach**. Together, **Netsach** and **Gevurah** can conceive **Tiferet**. Values, mating with power/energy, can produce the equilibrium and unity we understand as **Tiferet**. Isaac pleads with YHVH, the God-name for **Tiferet**, for Rivka (**Netsach**) to conceive. YHVH receives the plea, i.e., provides his input to enable the conception of **Tiferet**. Energy and power (**Gevurah**), which holds within it the potentiality for evil, can be tamed by combination with our innate ability to receive and recognize values (**Netsach**).

The sons struggle within Rivka (**Netsach**) and she questions YHVH (the potentiality for holiness leading to **Tiferet**) asking, *why am I?* -- What is the purpose of **Netsach**? YHVH responds, *"two nations are in your womb."* These are two potentialities, two divergent directions for humankind to take. Ultimately the younger will serve the elder. Perhaps *Torah* is alluding here to the struggle between and ultimate dominance of modern man over Neanderthals, Cro Magnons and other "brothers" in the process of evolution. Cro Magnons lived until 7000 to 8000 BCE as hunting and gathering people. They are believed to have died out when hunting gave way to crop cultivation and animal husbandry, a major step in the emergence of civilization. *The first came out red all over like a hairy mantle.* Sounds a bit like our image of a Cro Magnon or Neanderthal.

Afterward his brother came out and his hand held Esau's heel. That is, we humans developed on the heel of the hominids that preceded us. Through the age of Joseph, humankind begins to temper and civilize the more beast-like, **Gevurah**-based, evil side of human development.

The boys grew and Esau was a man knowing hunting, a man of the field. Jacob was a simple man living in tents. Esau, nicknamed *Edom,* red, becomes the hunter-gatherer. Jacob, named *on the heel of, follower*, becomes a shepherd and farmer.

As the story continues, Isaac, **Gevurah**, is ready to bless his first born Esau, but Jacob with the assistance of his mother, Rivka (**Netsach**), tricks Isaac into blessing Jacob instead. Civilization begins to take hold; the civilization movement is blessed over and above the hunter-gatherer peoples. As noted earlier, Rivka is associated in *The Zohar* with **Netsach**. In this part of the creation story Rivka breaks with tradition. She is guided by a sense of higher values, perhaps the values of civilization, of homo sapiens living together in tents, in societies, in cities, through **Netsach**.

In Kabbalistic terms, Esau/Edom represents isolated, unbalanced **Gevurah**. Edom, Esau's nickname, means red, the *Zohar*ic color symbol for **Gevurah**. Jacob also receives the flows from **Binah** and **Gevurah,** enabling him to farm and shepherd in contrast to his hunter brother, Esau. He similarly harnesses the forces of **Binah** to give him the intelligence, understanding and cunning to trick his brother out of his birthright and to receive the first son blessing from Isaac. Jacob's winning of the birthright symbolizes a primacy in unfolding creation of **Binah** over **Gevurah** and ultimately of **Tiferet** over the left side.

For the name *Jacob* is to Kabbalists a reference to the Sefirah **Tiferet**. As summarized in Figures 2 and 3 (Pages 21 & 23), and demonstrated in the previous two chapters, the Kabbalah associates each of the forefathers with different Sefirot. Abraham is the appellative for **Hesed**; Isaac is **Gevurah**; and Jacob is **Tiferet**. In the period of Abraham and Isaac, *Genesis* tells of the emanation of the Sefirot of **Hesed** and **Gevurah**. Now we enter the age of **Tiferet**. The blessing of **Tiferet** is introduced in Jacob's dream as translated below:

(Genesis 28:12-17) Jacob's Dream

*He (Jacob) dreamed and here, a ladder standing on earth and its head reaches heaven. And here, angels of Elohim ascend and descend on it. And here, YHVH (**Tiferet**) stood upon him and said, "I am YHVH, Elohim of Abraham (Hesed), your father, and Elohim of Isaac (Gevurah). The land that you lie on I shall give to you and to your seed. And your seed will be as the dust of the earth and you will spread seaward (westward) and forward (eastward) and northward and Negev-ward (southward). And all the families of the Earth will be blessed through you and through your seed. And here, I am with you. I shall guard you in everywhere that you go. I shall return you to this ground. Because I* *shall not leave you until I have made that of which I spoke to you."*

Jacob ended his sleep and said, "Surely there is YHVH in this place and I did not know." He feared and said, "how awesome is this place. This is none other than the house of Elohim and this is the gate of heaven."

In the dream Jacob sees the connection between heaven and earth, the Sefirot. The angels or messengers of Elohim **(Gevurah)** ascend and descend. YHVH (Tiferet) then appears, defining Himself as the God of **Hesed** and the God of **Gevurah**, the balance of **Hesed** and **Gevurah**.

In the blessing itself, the Kabbalistic directional symbols tell us that the power of **Tiferet,** the power of harmony and balance, will be with you as your seed influences the surrounding Sefirot. The seaward is **Yesod,** the forward is **Tiferet,** northward is **Gevurah** and Negev-ward is **Hesed**. And through **Tiferet** will be blessed all the families of the Earth. In a sense, harmony and balance is a definition of "blessing." All human beings can receive this emanation as can our communities, societies and nations, and be blessed. Blessing, as holiness, is an essence of **Tiferet**.

Tiferet develops through the course of the entire Joseph story. In the first scene, the tricking of Esau out of his blessing, Joseph is left side dominant. He is a creature of **Binah**. During his time in the East **(Tiferet),** Jacob matures his **Tiferet** centeredness as he grows his family and wealth in the land of Laban. This maturation of left-right balance culminates in his balanced dealings with Esau in the reunion, displaying **Hochma, Hesed** and **Netsach**. This re-encounter is preceded by the mysterious passage when he struggles with Elohim. Jacob's wrestling all night represents a personal struggle with the Sefirot. He sees the face of God and prevails. He has achieved Tiferet, he is renamed, **Israel**.

(Genesis 32: 25) Wrestling with Gevurah

And Jacob was left alone and a man struggled with him until the rising of dawn. And he saw that he could not overcome him and touched his thigh and Jacob's thigh was strained as he wrestled with him. And he said, "send me forth for dawn rises." And he said, "I will not send you unless you bless me." And he said to him, "What's your name?" And he said, "Jacob." And he said, "Not Jacob will you be called anymore, but Israel, because you wrestled with Elohim **(Gevurah)** *and with people and were able."*

Israel struggled with Elohim (**Gevurah/Din**) and achieved **Tiferet** blessing and balance.

Jacob can now confront Esau - the symbol of the bestial, Cro Magnon side of **Gevurah** - and prevail by introducing the force of **Tiferet** into the world. *Send me forth for the dawn rises.* What a beautiful metaphor for the creation of **Tiferet,** whose direction is East and whose heavenly body is the sun. *I will not send you unless you bless me.* We bless God (*Baruch Atah*) by striving to achieve **Tiferet** awareness and balance. *You have wrestled with Elohim and with people and were able.* We struggle in life with the left and right sides in our relationships with God and with people. If we are able, we achieve **Tiferet** blessing and balance, and our creation will be good.

Achieving balance, **Tiferet** blessing, and holiness is a struggle. It is a personal struggle for each of us as we personally wrestle with right and wrong, with the left and right forces of the Sefirot. If we prove able and achieve balance through **Tiferet**, we can truly also become co-creators and partners with God in holiness and blessing.

Chapter XI
Values, Emotion & Imagination - The Joseph Story

The Development of Yesod, the Creation of Keter

In the Kabbalah tradition, Joseph is the forefather representing the Sefirah **Yesod**. What does this mean and how does this association with **Yesod** open new interpretations of the Joseph story? What does this teach us about evil? These are the key questions addressed in this chapter.

The first part of the Joseph story, the saga of the striped or streaked coat, discloses the tension between **Netsach** and **Hod** and the balancing and mediating power and purpose of **Yesod**. This is a story about love, jealousy, hatred, pride and self-esteem on the one side, and principles and values counter-balancing on the other side. It is about the struggle we all experience between left and right in the world of Yetzirah.

The striped coat story is also about the creation of **Keter.** Joseph is the first person to "imagine." God has given Joseph and humankind the ability to dream and reflect on our dreams in a search for meaning. Through Joseph we are given the ability to feed new ideas into our Hochma and thus develop new and creative solutions from our imagination.

(Genesis 37: 1) – The Striped Coat Story

Jacob dwelt in the land where lived his fathers, in the land of Canaan. There are the generations of Jacob. Joseph was seventeen. He shepherded sheep with his brothers. He was young. He was with the son's of Bilhah and Zilpah, his father's women. Joseph brought their evil talk to his father. Israel loved Joseph more than all his sons for he was a son of his old age, and he made for him a striped coat. His brothers saw that their father loved him of all his brothers and they hated him and could not speak to him in peace.

Joseph dreamed a dream and he told his brothers and that added more. They hated him. And he said to them, "please listen to this dream that I dreamed. Here we are shearing sheaves within the field and here my sheaf woke up and also stood up. And here your sheaves came around and bowed to my sheaf." His brother said to him, "You shall surely reign over us and shall indeed have dominion over us?" They hated him even more for his dreams and for his words. And he dreamed still another dream. He told it to his brother. He said, "Here, I dreamed another dream and here the sun and the moon and eleven stars bowed to me." He told his father and his brothers and his father rebuked him. He said to him, "What is this dream that you dreamed. Indeed will it come that I and your mother and your brothers will bow to you toward the earth." His brothers envied him. His father guarded the thing.

His brothers went to feed their father's flock in Shechem. Israel said to Joseph, "Look, your brothers are shepherding in Shechem for you. I send you to them." And he said, "Here I am." And he said, "Please go see to the peace of your brothers and the peace of the sheep. And return with word."

He sent him from the valley of Hebron and he came toward Shechem. The man found him here wandering in the field. The man asked him, "what are you seeking?" He said, "I seek my brothers. Tell me please where do they shepherd?" And the man said, "They traveled from here, but I heard them say 'let's go toward Dotan (toward their *Dat*, religion, spirituality, knowledge*). And Joseph went following his brothers and he found them in Dotan.*

They saw him from far before he got close to them. They conspired against him for his death. They said to one another, "Here comes this master of dreams (imagination). And now come and let's kill him and throw him one of the pits and we'll say an evil animal ate him and we'll see what becomes of his dreams." And Reuben heard it and saved him from their hand and said, "Don't take a soul (life – Nefesh)." Reuben said to them, "Don't spill blood. Throw him in this

pit that's in the wilderness and don't extend a hand on him,"
in order that he would save him and return him to his father.

And it came to pass when Joseph came to his brothers, they
stripped Joseph, stripped his striped coat that was on him.
They grabbed him and they sent him toward the pit. The pit
was empty. There was no water in it. They sat to eat bread.
They lifted their eyes and saw and have a caravan of
Ishmaelites came from Gilead with their camels bearing
spices and balm and ladanum, going to carry toward Egypt.
Judah said to his brothers, " What profit if we kill our
brothers and hide his blood. Come let's sell him to the
Ishmaelites and our hand will not be on him, for he is our
brother, our flesh." And his brothers heard. Midianite men
passed by, merchants. They pulled and lifted Joseph from the
pit and they sold Joseph to the Ishmaelites for 20 silvers.
They brought Joseph toward Egypt.

Reuben returned to the pit and behold, no Joseph in the hole.
And he tore his clothes. He returned to his brother. He said,
"The boy is not and I, where do I come." They took Joseph's
coat and butchered a goat and dipped the coat in the blood.
They gashed the striped coat. They brought it to their father.
They said, "This we found. Do you know if this is the coat of
your son or not? And he knew it and said, "it is my son's
coat. An evil beast ate him. Torn in pieces is Joseph."
Jacob tore his robes and put a sack on his loins and mourned
many days for his son. All his sons and daughters rose to
calm him; he refused to be calmed and said, "I will go down
to my son in morning, toward Shaol" And his father cried for
him.

The Midianites sold him to Egypt to Potipar, officer of
Pharaoh, captain of the guard.

From a Kabbalistic reading, **Genesis** is about the ongoing
creation of the world. As Jacob is about the creation of **Tiferet** as a
balance between **Hesed** and **Gevurah**, Joseph is about the creation of
Yesod as a mediator between **Netsach** and **Hod**.

The word evil (*ra'ah*, also meaning bad) appears at the
beginning of the story. Joseph's first act is to recognize the evil talk

of his brothers, the sons of Bilhah and Zilpah, and bring it to his father, Jacob, **Tiferet**. A new force is introduced, the power to re-center evil talk. What is "evil talk?" It is talk devoid of principle and value (**Netsach**). It is talk based on emotions stimulated by our drives, instincts, and needs. At this stage, **Gevurah** is not involved, the talk is just talk, not acted on; but, as God warned Abel, "the opening for sin lies waiting." Joseph strives to neutralize the evil potentiality by bringing it to Jacob (**Tiferet**). **Tiferet** is the great modulator, the force for balance. Joseph (**Yesod**) is thus introduced as a "neutralizer" of our raw emotional side.

Talk planning a murder or other serious crime is certainly an example of "evil" talk. Such words, if not checked or balanced, could lead to the crime, the evil result. Does our society encourage or discourage the reporting of evil planning? Values enter the equation. Is the informer considered a tattler, a skunk, a snitch? Or is the reported seen as a savior, preventer, good citizen? Our value system, a system that is an emanation from God, determines the difference and endows us with the capability to balance the evil impulse or potentiality.

The story continues, *"Israel loved Joseph more than all his sons."* We recognize today that such favoritism in a parent's love, while natural, is the seed of powerful negative emotions, such as envy and jealousy. The unknowable source bestows us with a new kind of emotion, the love for our children. Love sits on the left side as an element of **Hod**. The all-encompassing emotion we feel for our own children is perhaps the most powerful motivator of all. Parents readily risk their lives for their children. Pure altruism comes from such love. It is an essential force to the survival of our species.

Yet, such a powerful force can also become a stimulus for sin. It is the majesty (**Hod**) of God that endows us with the gift of the capacity to love; yet, Jacob's out of balance love of Joseph stimulates action and reaction that creates strife and that throws the family out of balance. Jealousy is the result and ultimately, sin and evil.

"He made for him a striped coat." His brothers perceive that Jacob loves Joseph most, and a different element of **Hod** is aroused, hatred. *"They hated him and could not speak to him in peace,"* i.e.

the emotions of jealousy and hatred led to loss of **Yesod** balance, loss of 'peace.'

Hatred, jealousy and anger, like love, are forces that have enabled the survival and growth of civilization. When wronged we feel such strong emotions. These emotions stimulate us to defend ourselves, to fight for justice, good, and right. We fight to restore the higher principles and values of **Netsach.**

Yet jealousy and hatred are the foundation for sin. They are created as companions to love. Love stimulates the forces of jealousy and hatred. The hatred grows. Joseph tells his dreams and it fuels the hatred, it augments it. *"They hated him even more for his dreams and for his words." "His brother's envied him." "His father guarded the thing."* While emotion overwhelmed the brothers, Jacob, or **Tiferet,** is able to guard and control the *thing,* **Hod.**

God, the unknowable source in the ongoing process of creation, introduces a new force, the force of human values and communal principles. The force of **Netsach** appears as Jacob says, *"Look your brothers are shepherding for you."* They are doing your work. *"Go see to the peace of your brothers and the peace of the sheep."* Try to temper their hatred. Neutralize it through the power of **Yesod.** Serve as **Yesod** both to people and to animals.

It doesn't work. Emotion takes control. The brothers together have coalesced power (**Gevurah/Din**) and are able to act from their hatred. They *strip* Joseph. Stripping is a symbol of raw power and emotion. They throw him into a pit, a pit with no water (a symbol of **Hesed**). The **Gevurah - Hesed** pendulum becomes upset and leans heavily toward sin.

Judah argues, *"What profit if we kill our brother."* His capacity for reason, values and love emerges. **Binah, Hod, Hesed** and **Hochma** come into play.

Reuben returns too late and his emotions overcome him. He tears his clothes as a response to the emotions felt. God introduces the **Hod** motivators of love and grief. The brothers dip the striped coat in blood, a symbol of **Gevurah,** to cover their crime.

When brought before their father, Jacob concludes, *"An evil beast ate him."* Can beasts truly be evil? The word *ra'ah* appeared earlier, at the start of the story, as connected to talk with a potential for sin. Now Jacob refers to beasts with the potential for danger and death as "evil." Perhaps, *Torah* is telling us that evil should be seen as the natural potentiality for danger, death, and destruction - as something natural, yet controllable. We can overcome evil just as we can protect ourselves from wild beasts and from floods and storms (Noah). There is a connection between evil beasts and evil talk: both are evil in the sense of potentiality for sin from out-of-balance, out of control forces as a response to our felt needs. Need for love generates jealousy. Need for food generates hunger. If unchecked, animals and humans may act to satisfy their needs and, if not tempered by values, the result is evil.

Jacob then experiences his own **Hod** in the extreme in the form of a deep grief and refusal to be calmed. *"I will go down to my son in morning, toward Shaol."* Jacob recognizes he is leaning to the left, toward Shaol.

The coat of stripes has a double meaning. The Kabbalistic symbolism in the reading of the word commonly translated as *coat of many colors*. What is the significance of a coat and of colors, streaks or strips? This coat becomes the symbol of Joseph's distinction, of Jacob's love for him and of his special gifts. The Hebrew is mysterious. The word, *"ketonet,"* related to the word for cotton, also has within it *keter* and *natan* (given). If *ketonet* is understood as "endowed **Keter**" the story really comes alive with meaning.

Pursuant to this interpretation, the text reads, *"Israel loved Joseph more than all his sons for a son of his old age, he was to him. He will make for him an endowment of Keter.* The past tense can also be read as future for "make/create. And who is to do the making, God or Joseph or **Tiferet**? After this gift, Joseph becomes the dreamer and interpreter of dreams. He is becoming an imaginer, a child of **Keter**.

Joseph's dream that *"your sheaves came around and bowed to my sheaf"* now has added meaning. All the Sefirot and all creation bow down in honor and subservience to **Keter**. Keter is *Hamelech*, the king. The second dream, *"the sun and the moon and eleven stars bowed to me"* repeats the message that **Keter** is to be honored and its flows received by the sun, **Tiferet**, and the moon, **Malchut**, and the eleven brothers who become the tribes and priests of Israel. As

Albert Einstein noted, imagination is more important than knowledge. Imagination is the beginning of new knowledge and awareness.

When Joseph approaches, the brothers say, *"Here comes this master of dreams (imagination)."* They recognize Joseph's distinction as a receptacle for **Keter**, as one who can imagine. Understanding the coat as **Keter** the text can be interpreted: *And it came to pass when Joseph came to his brothers, they stripped Joseph, stripped his given **Keter** (striped coat - ketanto) that was on him.* The brothers stripped the **Keter** from **Yesod;** they stripped imagination from need awareness.

As the story continues, Joseph with **Yesod** and **Keter** is in route to Egypt to literally save the world. He uses his God-given gifts of **Hochma** and **Binah** to save civilization from the threat of natural disaster, from famine and starvation. He accomplishes this through a balance of **Hesed** and **Gevurah**, being motivated by a balance of **Netsach** and **Hod**. All the Sefirot come into play in the highly emotional, yet principle-driven reunion with his brothers. Joseph becomes the true symbol of center line balance: of **Yesod**, the balance between principles, purpose and emotions, of **Tiferet,** the balance between compassion and power, of **Da'at** and **Keter**, the balance between wisdom and understanding. In partnership with God, Joseph restructures and recreates society.

Joseph saves the world from starvation by perceiving and recognizing the problem through **Hochma**. Seeing the solution and convincing the authorities through **Binah,** exerting control and authority through **Din**, tempering that authority through **Hesed**, initiating and sustaining action through the self-motivating factors of **Netsach** and **Hod**. *Genesis* shows us the culminating effect of a **Keter**, **Tiferet** and **Yesod** balanced co-creator. Joseph demonstrates the role God plays in enabling us to interpret dreams, influence leaders, develop new ideas, and carry out our plans.

The culmination of the Joseph story comes when his brothers come for food to Egypt. Here, the interplay of **Gevurah/Din** and **Hesed** and of **Netsach** and **Hod** is inspiring and instructive. The brothers recognize their sin and "return" to balance. As noted earlier, in Judaism, repentance (*teshuvah*) is from the word "return." *Torah* teaches the essence of return in the Joseph story. With the help and guidance of Joseph, the brothers are able to turn away from sin. They are able to reflect with wisdom on the events of the past. Their right side is able to mediate. In contrast to the scene at the pit, their fundamental principles and values preside over their emotionality.

Joseph in his anonymous encounters with the brothers facilitates the re-balancing of his brothers' centerline. He enables them to attain a God awareness, to recognize their basic needs and define and articulate values and principles relative to those needs, to express their consciences, their sense of guilt for their past sins, to remember their sins and, when given the chance, to not repeat them. Joseph can thus accept their repentance, and rebuild the cohesiveness of the family.

The Joseph story illustrates the complete cycle of sin and repentance, of evil act and restoration of balance. It describes the source of the evil inclination, the jealousy, hatred, and resentment fostered by the unbalanced love from Jacob. The story describes the manifestation of the evil inclination, resulting in the near murder of Joseph and his sale into servitude. Finally, The Book of *Genesis* demonstrates the process of righting, of balancing and restoring, enabling repentance and community rebuilding. The Joseph story gives us a guide to restoring centerline balance, in society, in our family, in ourselves. God gives us the ability to repent as well as the potential for sin. God gives us the potential to fix the world, *Tikun Olam*.

Need Awareness and Yesod

To better understand **Yesod** and Joseph let's explore the psychology of need fulfillment and motivation. Abraham Maslow, a pioneer in the field of humanistic psychology, defined a hierarchy of needs. Human beings, according to Maslow, experience five levels of needs:

1. **Physiological Needs** - the need for food, shelter, warmth

2. **Safety/Security Needs** - the need to feel safe, the need for a sense of well being

3. **Affiliation, Recognition, and Social Needs** - a need for recognition, approval and belonging

4. **Self Esteem Needs** - the need to feel good about oneself, to feel competent and of value

5. **Self Actualization Needs** - the need for "peak experiences," the need for fulfilling a purpose or goal in life.

Understanding this hierarchy of needs has proven helpful to psychologists, teachers, ski instructors and others. This understanding of needs is also helpful in understanding ethics and sin. **Yesod** represents our ability to have and recognize needs. The other Sefirot assist us to satisfy these needs toward becoming creation partners.

Through a combination of left and right side forces, we can address our needs and wants. Unmet needs generate emotions in **Hod**. To ethically satisfy these needs requires a counter-balance of values and principles from **Netsach**. To the extent that need fulfillment requires the power and societal structure of **Gevurah/Din**, our degree of counter-balancing concern for others and compassion for those with greater need influences the ethical dynamic. **Hesed** gives us the impetus to help satisfy the needs of others rather than solely focus on our own. To ethically fulfill our needs in new, creative, innovative ways, we need a counter-balance to intelligence (**Binah**); we need imagination, wisdom and understanding: **Keter, Hochma** and **Binah**

Need awareness and the process of need fulfillment constitute a tenuous balance. If **Yesod** falls out of balance, we sin or act unethically. If our response is fully, totally and exclusively left side, our sin manifests as evil.

In the Joseph story a *Haya Ra'ah,* an evil animal, is the assumed cause of Joseph's demise. Here *Torah* introduces the concept of "evil". Evil is attributed to an animal guided only by its physiological needs - namely, hunger. Such an animal or human being, driven solely by its physiological needs - without the balance of principles and values - is defined as "evil".

Later in the Joseph story, hunger becomes the physiological basis for Joseph's opportunity to restructure Egyptian society and, like Noah, save the world. But unlike Noah, Joseph's **Hesed, Hochma** and **Netsach**- his right side- effectively modulates the powers of the left side. Joseph saves not just himself, but all peoples. In the process he builds a stronger society.

It is hunger, a physiological need that induces Jacob's sons to go down to Egypt to purchase food. In fact, Jacob does not allow the brothers to return a second time to Egypt until all the food is gone and hunger sets in, even though Shimon is left in captivity. Although not a sin, here is a question of ethics. Did Joseph violate his values in allowing Shimon to remain in prison, letting his love of and concern for Benjamin predominate? The ethical action might have been to do everything possible to free Shimon as quickly as possible. Instead, the need for safety and the companion emotion of fear directs Jacob.

A need for relationship as well as sexual drive motivates Potipar's wife to seduce Joseph. She unethically violates **Netsach** values relative to marital unfaithfulness and violation of trust. Due to her loss of pride and self-esteem, strong emotions surely motivated her gravely unethical act of false accusation. She is rejected. Rejection causes humiliation. Humiliation brings anger and the urge for revenge. The result is the false accusation of Joseph.

The need for self-esteem manifests in Joseph's early dealings with his brothers and perhaps further explains their sin in seizing and selling their brother. Jealousy is the emotion we feel when a competitor or peer undermines our self-esteem. Jealousy and anger connect within the brothers and result in sin.

The need for self-actualization can also become a strong motivator. The stick-to-it-ness we feel based on accomplishment and the high we experience from success are manifestations of satisfying this self-actualization need.

However, self-actualization lacking **Netsach, Hesed** and/or **Hochma** is doomed to become unethical. Many politicians and leaders, in contrast to Joseph, do not recognize that our abilities and solutions come from God. Their self-actualizing motivation stems from self-centered egoism. Their emotion-laden agenda is opportunistic. Unlike Joseph, they lack core values, concern for others and wisdom to grasp the larger picture.

Chapter XII
Exploring the Balance in Ourselves

During the Ten Days of Penitence, the period from Rosh Hashanah through Yom Kippur, Jews look back on the past year, take measure of the course of their lives, identify their sins, ask for forgiveness for their sins and ask God for atonement. To Kabbalists, Rosh Hashanah is a commemoration of creation, the start of a process that is ongoing and, in which, we play a major role as partners with God. Hopefully, the Kabbalistic tradition and the concepts of evil, sin and ethics explored in this book can add a new depth and meaningfulness for us as we assess our personal role as partners in creation.

As I asked our congregation in Rosh Hashanah services this past week, reflect for a moment on the balance of left and right in your own lives. All of us struggle to stay balanced. Let's focus on the three Sefirotic continuums as depicted below.

Binah	←→	**Hochma**
Gevurah	←→	**Hesed**
Hod	←→	**Netsach**

It's almost like a seesaw as we try to stay balanced. Focus on your wisdom, your gift from God. When have you recently demonstrated insightful wisdom? Performed a wise act? Made a wise decision? Thought of a wise solution? Come up with a new and novel idea or approach? Were you smart enough to carry out your insight? Has your understanding and intelligence enabled you to develop your wisdom in a balanced and positive manner? Were you "wise in understanding," as Sefer Yetzirah teaches? Can you think of instances where your understanding or intelligence ran off with ideas that were not so wise, perhaps even foolish?

On the **Gevurah** ←→ **Hesed** continuum, think for a moment about the fundamental goodness in you. It is a gift from God, a flow from the Source. How has this **Hesed** helped you? Helped your friends and family and co-workers and employees?

Now, think about your power. Has it been corrupting as for Moses, culminating in the extermination of the Midianites? Have we acted on our power over others without **Hesed**? Have we created through strength, money, and energy without sufficient good intention, positive purpose, higher mission, or altruism? Were we selfish or other oriented?

Finally, on the **Hod** ←→ **Netsach** continuum, how have we fared? With respect to **Netsach**, how have our God-given values and principles directed us at home, at work, in our communities? Have we stuck to our principles in emotionally testing times? Have we preserved and strengthened our values in the face of our personal needs and conflicting emotions? Do we have enough motivation to carry out our life mission(s)? Are we becoming lazy or stuck? Have we given up?

With respect to **Hod,** have we sinned by reacting emotionally rather than rationally? What was the consequence? How do we set it right? Have we, like Joseph's brothers, acted on our hatred and jealousy; or have we, like the mature Joseph, been able to overcome our emotions, focus on our values and been able to forgive and restore community, reunite family and help achieve a balance of need fulfillment in ourselves and those with whom we interact and love?

We have the capability to feel the flow of energies into the 10 ever-reacting, ever dynamic Sefirot in ourselves. If we can get in touch with these creative, Divine flows on Rosh Hashanah, Yom Kippur, Sukkot, Tu Bishvat, Pesach, the counting of the omer, Shavuot, Rosh Hodesh, and Shabbat, we can feel and experience God. These creation-focused, partnering-focused holidays are opportunities to understand evil, to understand sin, to understand repentance and to become more spiritual and balanced human beings.

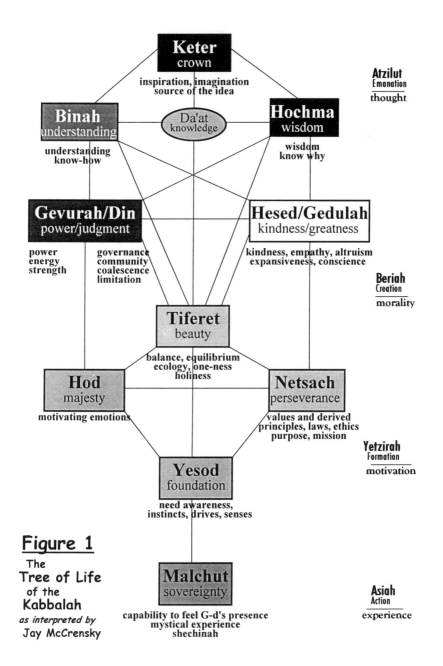

Figure 1
The
Tree of Life
of the
Kabbalah
as interpreted by
Jay McCrensky

109

FIGURE 2
DECIPHERING THE ZOHAR AND OTHER KABBALISTIC WORKS
Metaphors, Symbols and Appellatives

The Sefirot: Colors, rivers, heavens, supports, worlds, aspects, borders, hosts, levels, powers, sides, areas, lights, garments, steps, crowns, foundations, streams, gates, the Garden of Eden, the chariot, field of apple trees, Adam Kadmon.

Keter Hochma, Binah: The undisclosed.

Hesed, Gevurah, Tiferet, Netsach, Hod, Yesod: The six days, the sun, the Lebanon, vav.

Hesed to Yesod [in some writings, **Hochma** to Yesod]: Ze'ir Anpin (the impatient one, the small face)

Simeon Bar Yohai: Sacred lamp.

Keter (crown): King, black, no color, will, nothingness, well, Israel, most hidden One, hidden upper light, most mysterious, Arikh Anpin (the patient one, the large face), ancient of days, Ehyeh (I will be), Atika Kadisha (ancient holy one).

Hochma (wisdom): Yod, dark blue, father, husband, first point, beginning (reshit), brain, Yah.

Binah (understanding): First heh, green, mother, wife, sea, palace, basin, womb, heart, brain, inner voice, Leah, YHVH vocalized as Elohim.

Hesed (kindness), Gedulah (greatness): Upper waters, white, south, right arm, Abraham, Miriam. hasid, El.

Gevurah (strength), Din (judgment): Lower waters, red, north, left arm, fire, wine, the evil serpent, the accuser, the tempter, Isaac, Elohim.

Tiferet (beauty), Rehamim (mercy): vav, Holy One Blessed be He (Hakadosh Baruch Hu), Holy King, yellow, son, sun, torso, heart, east, wind, tree of life, written Torah, prince, central pillar, central column, Jacob, YHVH.

Netsach (victory, endurance): the right leg, Moses, Rebecca, YHVH Tzevaot.

Netsach and Hod: the two pillars, willows of the brook, testicles.

Hod (majesty): the left leg, Aaron, Sarah, Elohim Tzevaot.

Yesod (foundation): Tzadik (righteous one), kol (all), phallus, Joseph, Tamar, moon, Shaddai, El Hai.

Malchut (sovereignty): second heh, community of Israel, Shechinah, queen, Sabbath, the female, bride, princess, the daughter, moon, blue, west, great sea, speech, oral Torah, end of thought, lower mother, tree of knowledge, apple orchard, Kind David, Rachel, Miriam, Esther, Adonoi, *Tzedek* (righteousness), Tzedakah (charity), liver, feet, mouth.

About the Author

Jay McCrensky has studied and taught Kabbalah for over 20 years. In addition to teaching diverse Kabbalah, Siddur, *Torah* and Jewish Holidays courses, he leads a weekly Kabbalah study group and lectures widely for congregations, religious schools, psychological societies, universities and other groups interested in Kabbalah, spirituality, Jewish mysticism and the issue of evil. A member of the Fabrangen Havurah in Washington, DC, his Jewish education includes studies at the Hebrew University and Hebrew Union College Jewish Institute of Religion. His degrees are in philosophy from the University of Rochester, and management (MBA) from Stanford University.

The author is President of Marketshare, Inc. (an association management and marketing consulting firm); director of the Machaya Klezmer Band (bassist, accordionist and the originator of Klezmer Dance); Vice President of marketing at Dovetail Technologies (an emerging biopharmaceutical company) and a professional ski instructor at Whitetail